ROE AND WADE:
History of Roe and Wade, Overturning of Roe and Wade and Its Dissenting Opinions.

Grace Roberts

Table Of Contents

THE ROE AND WADE RULE'S HISTORY

The turbulent background of the important Roe v. Wade decision

Two public health crises that resulted in miscarriages and serious health issues for newborn infants in the 1960s increased support for abortion, paving the way for the famous U.S. Supreme Court decision.

In April 1970, Jane Hodgson took up the phone, dialed her neighborhood police, and requested that they place her under arrest.

The Minnesota doctor had earlier that day conducted an abortion on a 24-year-old mother of three who had rubella, a condition linked to miscarriage, newborn mortality, and serious health issues for children who survive pregnancy. Like many other states, Minnesota only permitted "therapeutic abortions," which ended pregnancies only in cases when the mother's life was in danger.

Hodgson had seen patients begging for unlicensed abortions and suffering, even dying, when they got them from other, incompetent physicians. She said that she "had to make a decision between obeying the current law or fulfilling her commitment to her patient, her profession, and her society" in an affidavit to the grand jury that indicted her.

Here's a look at the time leading up to the historic rulings, what those two cases included, and their significance in light of the upcoming Supreme Court decision that is anticipated to overturn decades of precedent supporting the right to end a pregnancy.

***Examining the country's restrictions
on abortion.***

Although there was no resistance to
abortion in the early years of the country,
this changed in the late 19th century when it
started to become more taboo. It was
likewise forbidden by the middle of the 20th
century. By the late 1960s, abortions were a
crime in almost every state, despite the fact
that women often sought and obtained
them. These laws provided few, if any,
exceptions for the mother's health or
situations involving rape and incest.

However, two public health emergencies
during that time period opened up the
abortion discussion. The first was
thalidomide, a medication sold in Europe as
a treatment for anxiety, insomnia, and
morning sickness. Thalidomide caused
hundreds of women to miscarry and around
10,000 kids born throughout the globe

suffered serious physical abnormalities. As a result, the drug's producers withdrew it.

Sherri Finkbine, an American actress best known for playing "Miss Sherri" on the children's television program Romper Room, unintentionally used the medication early in her pregnancy even though it was never permitted in the United States. She offered a newspaper interview after being made aware that she had used the substance in an effort to raise awareness of its risks. She had requested anonymity, but once the tale went viral, neither her hospital nor any other institution would perform an abortion.

To get the abortion, a trip to Sweden would be necessary. A 1962 Gallup survey found that the majority of Americans agreed with Finkbine's choice, despite the criticism she received from the general public, the death threats she received, and the fact that she lost her job.

When the rubella virus, commonly known as German measles, was on the rise in the middle of the 1960s, support for abortion increased. Rubella-infected pregnant women started having miscarriages. An estimated 20,000 newborns were born with congenital anomalies include deafness, unusual anatomy, intellectual difficulties, and cardiac issues; many newborn babies died as a result. Despite the fact that many physicians, including Hodgson, supported abortions for expectant women who had rubella, the majority of states' anti-abortion legislation placed them in fear of arrest, license revocation, and other consequences.

Two test cases that might change American abortion legislation were being heard in American courts while the abortion debate raged.

The constitutional right to privacy and Jane Roe Norma McCorvey, at age 21, got pregnant in 1969. She was expecting her third kid, however she chose not to raise either child due to financial difficulties and drug problems. She wanted an abortion this time. McCorvey, however, resided in Texas, which forbade abortions unless the mother's life was in danger, despite the fact that several states had started to significantly liberalize their abortion regulations.

McCorvey could not afford to leave the state or have a covert abortion from a reputable doctor, unlike richer and more resourceful women. However, she had heard of two lawyers who were interested in filing a test case with a client similar to her—someone whose age and social standing would highlight the injustice of abortion regulations.

McCorvey consented to take part in a case brought by lawyers Linda Coffee and Sarah Weddington. The complaint was submitted under the fictitious name Jane Roe, which is often used in cases when a woman wants to hide her identity. Her legal team filed a lawsuit against Henry Wade, the district attorney of the county where "Jane Roe" resided, claiming that Texas' legislation infringed on women's fundamental right to privacy, which gives them the ability to conduct their lives without excessive governmental meddling.

A panel of three judges from the U.S. District Court concurred and declared the Texas legislation unconstitutional. Wade refused to cease pursuing physicians, and the court rejected to force Texas to stop using the outdated legislation. McCorvey finally gave birth a third time and put the kid up for adoption while her case was being heard in court.

Mary Doe enlarges on her point:

Another test case, Doe v. Bolton, was proceeding in the meanwhile. Sandra Bensing, a 22-year-old Georgian who was expecting her fourth child in 1970, made the decision that she wanted an abortion. She was married but seeking a divorce since she was having problems raising her children, who were all adopted or in foster care.

Georgia at the time prohibited abortion except in situations where the mother's life was in danger or there was a chance of a permanent handicap; in rape cases; or in situations where a fetus was likely to be born with a serious anatomical abnormality or mental disability. A almost overwhelming burden of evidence accompanied each prospective restriction. For instance, a woman who had been raped had to record the incident, and her friends or relatives may file a lawsuit to prevent her from receiving the surgery.

Attorneys from the Legal Aid Society and the American Civil Liberties Union selected Bensing as a test case and sued Georgia attorney general Arthur Bolton when a hospital refused to provide her a therapeutic abortion. The attorneys said that the statute violated "Mary Doe's" constitutional right to privacy and self-determination, impeded medical personnel from doing their duties, and that "Mary Doe" should not only have had the abortion permitted because of a psychological impairment.

Bensing ultimately had an abortion in a private facility that was exempt from the same regulations as the public hospital, but the case was still pursued. A three-judge District Court panel ruled in 1970 that women had the right to get abortions even if they had not been sexually assaulted, were not in imminent danger of dying, and were not carrying fetuses that may suffer serious health issues. While adding that governments had a legitimate interest in monitoring abortion as part of their obligation to safeguard life, including fetuses, the decision also decided that limits on abortions during the first trimester infringed women's private rights.

The Supreme Court's Roe v. Doe case

The fate of both cases, as well as the availability of abortion in the US, rested in the hands of the US Supreme Court in 1973.

In 1971 and 1972, Weddington argued Roe v. Wade before the US Supreme Court. At the time of the opening oral argument, she was just 26 years old, and this was the first case she had ever tried in court. She claimed that abortions were a personal choice and that the courts were women's only option when states like Texas outlawed them. She made her argument in front of the all-male judges.

She emphasized the risk of pregnancy and delivery and referred to abortion as "an essential choice" in women's personal lives. Weddington said that one of the most defining parts of a woman's life is probably becoming pregnant. Her body is disturbed by it. Her schooling is hampered by it. She loses her job as a result. And it often interferes with her whole family life.

Roe v. Wade and Doe v. Bolton were both decided by the Supreme Court on the same day. On January 22, 1973, it was determined in Roe that a woman's constitutional right to privacy extends to her choice to end her pregnancy. It also determined that governments had an interest in safeguarding both pregnant women and "the potentiality of human life," enabling them to control abortion practices beyond the first trimester of pregnancy and impose standards on matters like the training of abortionists. States might forbid the treatments during the third trimester as long as their laws included exception for the mother's life or continuous health.

The court stated in Doe that "a woman's constitutional right to an abortion is not absolute," but that it was too onerous to need several doctors or whole hospital committees to rule on the necessity of an abortion. The court also determined that abortions judged required to preserve women's health—which might encompass "any physical, emotional, psychological, family, and the women's age relevant to the well-being of the patient"—could not be prohibited by states at any stage of pregnancy.

Reaction to the decisions

In a single stroke, the Supreme Court invalidated the laws of 46 states and overturned a century's worth of abortion prohibitions. However, the first reaction to the historic ruling was muted and overshadowed by other political concerns. Numerous Protestant leaders either voiced their unequivocal approbation of the decision or did not publicly react to it. However, Catholic bishops promptly voiced unprecedented opposition, and within weeks, local anti-abortion organizations that had been opposing state-level liberalization legislation organized into a nationwide campaign determined to have the verdicts overturned.

American women reacted in large numbers at the same time. Prior to Roe v. Wade, estimates indicated that there were around 130,000 illegal abortions performed in the United States annually; but, as Center for Disease Control statistics have shown, following that decision, the number fell to 17,000 in 1975. They claimed that "with the ongoing rise in legal abortion services, illegal abortion may soon be practically eliminated as a cause of death" since the number of women whose deaths were officially proven to have been caused by an illegal abortion decreased from 39 in 1972 to three in 1975.

By 1980, there were around 1.6 million abortions carried out annually in the United

States. With time, the technique improved in safety, accessibility, and cost; it was also made available as an outpatient operation in freestanding clinics as opposed to merely hospitals.

The doctor who disobeyed Minnesota law, Hodgson, never went to prison and her sentence was overturned as a result of Roe and Doe. She performed abortions throughout the remainder of her career while campaigning to advance women's reproductive health despite harassment for her outspoken position.

The U.S. Supreme Court formally overturned Roe v. Wade on Friday, concluding that the constitutional right to an abortion, sustained for over 50 years, is no longer valid.

Justice Samuel Alito, who penned the majority opinion for the court, stated that the 1973 Roe decision and subsequent high court decisions affirming it "must be overruled" because they were "egregiously wrong," the arguments were "exceptionally weak," and they were so "damaging" that they amounted to "an abuse of judicial authority."

The ruling, the majority of which was made public in early May, implies that abortion rights will be immediately restricted in over half of the states, with other limitations certain to follow. Abortion won't really be accessible in a sizable portion of the nation. The ruling may also imply that both the court and the abortion debate will be in the spotlight throughout the forthcoming autumn elections as well as throughout the rest of the year.

The future of reproductive rights in America and ROE v. Wade

What could daily living be like in an America post-Roe?

Justice Clarence Thomas, chosen by the first President Bush, and the three Justices Trump selected—Justices Neil Gorsuch, Brett Kavanaugh, and Amy Coney Barrett—joined the Alito decision. President George W. Bush's choice for chief justice, Chief Justice John Roberts, agreed solely in the ruling and would have confined the ruling to maintaining the Mississippi legislation at issue in the case, which forbade abortions beyond 15 weeks. Both the majority and the dissent demonstrated "a persistent freedom from uncertainty on the legal question that I cannot share," he added, describing the ruling as "a significant shock to the legal system."

Justices Sonia Sotomayor and Elena Kagan, both nominated by President Obama, as well as Justice Stephen Breyer, who was selected by President Clinton, dissented. According to the, "young women today will come of age with less rights than their mothers and grandparents," as a result of the court judgment. They did state that the court's ruling indicates that "A woman has no rights whatsoever beginning with conception. Even at the greatest personal and family expense, the state has the power to order women to carry a pregnancy to term."

We dissent, they said, "with regret for this Court, but more so for the many millions of American women who now have lost a basic constitutional right."

Alito's decision is a masterful synthesis of the many Roe objections that have long been present in academics.

No authority is left uncited in Alito's 78-page opinion, which has a 30-page appendix, to support the idea that certain constitutional clauses do not grant an inherent right to privacy or personal autonomy. Similarly, there is no proof that people's reliance on court precedents on abortion over the past 50 years should matter.

Alito cited the 1992 judgment in Planned Parenthood v. Casey, which was authored by Justices Sandra Day O'Connor, Anthony Kennedy, and David Souter, all of whom were Republican appointments to the court and supported the fundamental principle of Roe. In the Casey judgment, the author "conceded" that reliance interests were not actually at issue since contraception could nearly always prevent unintended births. Alito drew attention to this statement.

The campaign to restrict access to abortion is about to reach its peak. But it started long before Roe.

The 1992 judgement, however, went on to call that same claim "unrealistic" because it "refuse[s] to confront the reality]" that for decades, "people have formed personal relationships and made decisions... in dependence on the availability of abortion in the event that contraceptive should fail." Not quite the concession Alito referred to.

Justices often choose statements at random, but they shouldn't be taken out of context or from living former coworkers; doing so makes them uncomfortable.

But ultimately, Alito's viewpoint serves a more significant purpose—or maybe even many purposes.

He wrote for the majority and said unequivocally that states and their citizens should determine whether or not to legalize abortion. We believe that the Constitution does not provide a right to an abortion, he wrote.

Any state regulation of abortion is presumed to be valid, according to Alito, and "must be sustained if there is a rational basis on which the legislature could have thought" it was serving "legitimate state interests," such as "respect for and preservation of prenatal life at all stages of development," in the event that it is challenged.

He further said that states have the right to control abortion in order to stop "gruesome and barbarous" medical practices, "preserve the integrity of the medical profession," and stop discrimination based on a person's race, sex, or handicap, including banning abortion in situations of fetal abnormalities. In the end, all of that means that states seem to have total discretion over whether or not to outlaw abortions.

A procedure that permits minors to have abortions may no longer exist now that Roe has been overturned.

Alito made an effort to ease concerns about the scope of his conclusion towards the end of Friday's ruling. "We stress that our decision only pertains to the constitutional right to abortion and not any other right in order to prevent our choice from being misinterpreted or mischaracterized. Nothing in this ruling should be interpreted as challenging earlier decisions that do not deal with abortion."

However, Justice Thomas stated in his concurring opinion that the legal justification for Friday's decision could be used to reverse other significant decisions, such as those that legalized gay marriage, prohibited the criminalization of consensual homosexual behavior, and protected married people's rights to access contraception.

Because of this, all of those precedents "should be given another look in future instances." mainly because they are "demonstrably false."

The court's liberals emphasized that Alito's assurances at the conclusion of his opinion that this ruling was actually exclusively about abortion were called into question by Thomas's phrasing.

Justice Thomas' concurrence, which makes it apparent that he disagrees with the program, poses the first issue with the majority's assessment, according to what they wrote. Nothing in today's ruling, according to Justice Thomas, "casts doubt on non-abortion precedents," he clarifies, "meaning only that they are not at issue in this particular case."

The following stages on abortion in the nation will take many different forms, virtually all of which will culminate in abortion bans.

Many states still have abortion restrictions in place, including Mississippi, North Carolina, and Wisconsin. If Roe is overturned, these states may return to the way things were before Roe. Such states' officials can try to enforce outdated laws or urge the courts to revive them. A 1931 Michigan statute, for instance, would classify abortion as a crime. Democratic governor Gretchen Whitmer has been attempting to overturn that rule.

A string of recently enacted state legislation "Trigger bans," more recent legislation that anti-abortion rights politicians pushed through in several states in anticipation of the Supreme Court's decision, provide another route to outlawing abortion. According to CRR and Guttmacher, there are similar laws in effect in around 15 states, however they are divided into several groups and are located in the South, West, and Midwest.

Abolishing abortion will happen swiftly in several states. New research from the Guttmacher Institute reveals that South Dakota, Kentucky, and Louisiana had statutes in place that legislators specifically intended to go into force the moment the Roe judgment was overturned. Similar legislation exist in Idaho, Tennessee, and Texas, where most abortions are already prohibited after six weeks of pregnancy. These laws would go into effect after 30 days. According to Guttmacher, seven other "trigger ban" states have legislation that call for governors or attorneys general to take action in order to enforce them.

Susan B. Anthony Pro-Life America's state policy director Sue Liebel said she anticipates authorities in many of those Republican-controlled states would move quickly to do so.

According to Liebel, "We have been talking to all of them about acting right away." "In that case, let's be prepared. How are you going to bring it back?"

A lot of states have recently implemented laws that prohibit abortion at different stages of pregnancy, known as gestational bans. Many of such laws have been overturned by courts in response to legal challenges, including those that prohibit abortions beyond six weeks of pregnancy in Georgia, Ohio, and Idaho. Now, such laws may go into action right now. The same might be said about a recent Oklahoma legislation that makes conducting an abortion a crime that carries a jail sentence.

The Center for Reproductive Rights' senior director of litigation, Julie Rikelman, predicted a significant shift in a very short amount of time. This term, Rikelman represented the Center in its Supreme Court appeal against Mississippi's ban on abortion.

There may be a number of additional limitations that affect where, by whom, and under what circumstances abortions may be performed. A few examples are legislation requiring parental notice or approval for abortions involving underage patients; various health rules for physicians and clinics; and other restrictions that many medical organizations claim are pointless, costly, and challenging to comply with.

These three Supreme Court rulings may be in jeopardy if Roe v. Wade is reversed.

Could Roe v. Wade's overthrow have effects that go beyond abortion?

Last but not least, Liebel said that some governors should think about convening extra sessions to adopt new laws in reaction to the decision.

According to legal experts, the court's judgment will provide new issues for other courts to resolve, including how to apply the precise wording of the decision to other state laws.

In the immediate aftermath of the judgment, states around the nation would see "legal anarchy," according to Rikelman, an attorney with the Center for Reproductive Rights.

Rikelman predicted that rather than fewer litigation, "we will see substantially more litigation in the federal courts."

There are a number of abortion restrictions in place in several states, including Texas and Oklahoma, raising the issue of whether ones are really legal. These statutes all have various clauses and punishments, which might cause confusion and lead to more legal disputes in state and federal courts.

SBA Pro-Life America's Liebel recognized that more legal disputes are anticipated.

"To be honest, that will return us to our original position. Each side attempts to step right on the line and go beyond what is acceptable, "said Liebel.

State court battles are also possible. Despite how the US Supreme Court has interpreted the US Constitution, several state constitutions may include safeguards for abortion rights. For instance, the American Civil Liberties Union and other reproductive rights organizations are contesting a 15-week abortion ban in Florida on the grounds that it violates the safeguards for private rights granted by the state constitution. The legislation is fashioned after the one in Mississippi.

Following the historic Supreme Court arguments, the future of Roe v. Wade is in jeopardy.

Following the historic Supreme Court arguments, the future of Roe v. Wade is in jeopardy.
Rikelman mentions the Texas statute known as S.B. 8, which went into force in September, even without overturning Roe. The bill depends on people bringing civil lawsuits to enforce an abortion ban, and it has inspired other copycat measures in other states, including Oklahoma.

Battles for interstate enforcement.

States that limit abortion rights will probably also enact abortion bans, according to Rikelman. She mentions that some state legislators are attempting to make it illegal for individuals to perform abortions on citizens of other states.

States and state politicians are already having an influence on people's access to abortion in areas where it would still be allowed, she said.

For instance, a supermajority of Republicans in Kentucky passed an omnibus abortion law earlier this year that adds a number of new regulations for dispensing medication abortion pills and calls for extraditing individuals from other states who knowingly provide abortion pills to residents of Kentucky. The enforceability of such kinds of legislation is questionable.

In the meanwhile, several states are working to make abortions more accessible in anticipation of an increase in the number of patients coming from states with tight laws to have operations. This year, Connecticut legislators approved legislation aimed at shielding abortion providers from out-of-state legal action.

Rikelman added, "This simply creates a whole variety of difficulties. The U.S. Supreme Court might possibly get involved in "all of those distinct conflicts," which will need to be resolved through the legal system.

Leah Litman, a law professor at the University of Michigan, notes that the anti-abortion movement will not be happy with this victory. In an interview, she said, "A nationwide abortion ban will be on the table the next time the Republicans gain control of the Senate, White House, and House of Representatives."

The Guttmacher Institute states that the long-term drop in abortions has reversed, despite the fact that abortions have now generally become much more limited. 930,160 abortions were performed in the United States in 2020, which is an 8 percent rise from 2017. The Institute also noted that fewer individuals were becoming pregnant at the same period, and of those who did, a greater percentage decided to have an abortion.

Dissenting opinion of the Supreme Court in favor of overturning Roe v. Wade

On Friday, June 24, 2022, the Supreme Court overturned Roe v. Wade and Planned Parenthood of Southeastern Pennsylvania v. Casey, declaring that the Constitution does not guarantee a right to abortion. The states were given back control over abortion laws and access.

Roe v. Wade, 410 U.S. 113 (1973), and Planned Parenthood of Southeastern Pennsylvania v. Casey, 505 U.S. 833 (1992), have safeguarded the freedom and equality of women for half a century. The Supreme Court ruled in Roe, and Casey upheld it, that a woman's freedom to choose whether or not to become a mother is protected by the Constitution. Roe established, and Casey upheld, that the government could not decide a woman's course of action during the first trimester of her pregnancy.

The government had no power over a woman's body or the path of her life; it had no say in what the lady would do in the future. See Gonzales v. Carhart, 550 U.S. 124, 171-172 (2007) and Casey, 505 U.S. at 853. (Ginsburg, J., dissenting). Giving a woman meaningful control over this very personal and important life decision required respecting her autonomy and affording her complete equality.

The difficulties and polarization of the abortion debate were both well known to Roe and Casey. The Court was aware that American opinion on the "moral[ity]" of "terminating a pregnancy, even at its earliest stage" is profoundly divided. 505 U. S. Casey, at 850. The Court also acknowledged that "the State has legitimate interests" in defending the "life of the fetus that may become a child" "from the start of the pregnancy." Id., at 846.

Therefore, as is often the case when values and aims clash, the Court established a balance. It was decided that the State had the right to outlaw abortions after fetal viability as long as there were safeguards in place to protect the life or health of the mother. It maintained that the State might restrict abortion in a variety of significant ways even before viability. But the Court ruled that up until the viability threshold was reached, a State could not place a "substantial impediment" in the way of a woman's "right to chose the procedure" as she (and not the government) saw fit, taking into account all the details and complexity of her individual life. Ibid. The Court does away with that equilibrium today. It claims that a woman has no legal standing whatsoever beginning with fertilization. Even at the highest personal and family sacrifices, a State has the power to compel women to carry a pregnancy to term. The majority maintains that an abortion limitation is legal whenever it is reasonable, which is the least amount of legal examination possible.

Additionally, because the Court has often said that it is logical to preserve fetal life, States will feel free to adopt any kind of limitations. Abortions are illegal in Mississippi after the 15th week of pregnancy, according to the relevant statute. However, according to the majority's decision, a different State's legislation may do so after ten weeks, or five, or three, or one—or, once again, from the time of fertilization. In preparation for today's decision, states have already approved similar legislation. There will be more. Some States have passed legislation that covers all types of abortion procedures, including home medication abortions. Without making any allowances for situations when a woman is the victim of rape or incest, laws have been created.

A woman will be forced to carry her rapist's kid or a young girl's father's child under such regulations, regardless of whether doing so would ruin her life. After today's decision, certain States may also force women to carry fetuses with severe physical defects to term, such as those with Tay-Sachs disease who are certain to pass away within a few years after birth.

States may even contend that there is no need for a woman to be protected from the danger of death or bodily damage where abortion is prohibited. A State will be allowed to force a woman to have a child by coercing her to give birth in a variety of situations.

Additionally, it will mainly be up to the States to decide how to enforce all of these harsh prohibitions. Of course, a State has the legal authority to charge abortion providers with crimes and sentence them to long jail terms. Some States, though, won't stop there. After today's ruling, it's possible that a state legislation may criminalize the woman's actions as well, imprisoning or fining her for having the audacity to seek or procure an abortion. And as Texas has shown, a State may set its people against one another in an endeavor to apprehend anybody who attempts to get an abortion or helps another person do so.

The majority makes an effort to conceal the impact of its holding's geographic reach. The majority claims that today's ruling allows "any State" to treat abortion as they see fit. At 79, ante. Of course, it offers little solace to the unfortunate lady who cannot afford to go to a far-off State for treatment. Women with little financial means will be most harmed by today's judgment. In any case, there will soon be interstate limits as well.

Following this ruling, certain States may prohibit women from accessing abortion drugs or going outside of their state to have an abortion. Some may make it illegal to assist women seek abortion services in other States by giving them information or funds.

The most concerning aspect of the ruling is that it contains no wording that would prevent the federal government from outlawing abortions countrywide, once again starting at the time of conception and without making any exceptions for rape or incest. In such case, "the opinions of [a State's] people" will not be significant. Ante, one. The difficulty for a lady will be finding the money to go to Toronto rather than "New York [or] California." at 4 ante (KAVANAUGH, J., concurring).

Whatever the specifics of the new regulations, one outcome of today's decision is certain: women's rights and their position as free and equal citizens will be restricted. Yesterday, the Constitution ensured that a woman facing an unintended pregnancy might choose whether to have a child, with all the life-altering implications such action entails, on her own terms (within appropriate bounds). The Constitution also preserved "the capacity of women to participate equally in [this Nation's] economic and social life" by preserving each woman's right to choose her own reproductive options. 505 U.S. at 856; Casey. but not anymore.

This Court maintains that a State may nonetheless compel a woman to become pregnant, outlawing even the earliest abortions. Thus, a State has the power to turn something that, when done freely, is amazing, into something that, when forced, may be a nightmare. Some women, particularly wealthy ladies, will discover methods to resist the state's exercise of authority. Others won't be as lucky—those without money, childcare, or the capacity to take time off from work.

They might attempt an unsafe abortion method and suffer physical harm or even pass away. They could get pregnant and give birth, but it will probably come at a high personal or family cost. They will pay a price in terms of losing control over their life, at the very least. The majority of people now believe that despite the Constitution's pledges of equality and freedom for everyone, it will not act as a shield.

And nobody should believe that this majority's work is complete. The correct Roe and Casey recognition is not sufficient on its own. On the contrary, the Court has consistently connected it to other firmly established liberties regarding sexual orientation, gender identity, and family connections. Most clearly, the freedom to access and use contraception led directly to the freedom to end a pregnancy. Griswold v.

Connecticut (381 U.S. 479), Eisenstadt v. Baird (405 U.S. 438), and others (1972). Later, such rights opened the door for same-sex marriage and intimate rights. See Obergefell v. Hodges, 576 U. S. 644; Lawrence v. Texas, 539 U. S. 558 (2003). (2015).

They are all woven into the same constitutional framework, which safeguards individual autonomy over even the most intimate life choices. Today, the majority is quick to assure us that nothing it does "cast[s] doubt on precedents that do not involve abortion," or, to be more precise, "most of it." Compare ante, at 66, with ante, at 3 (concurring THOMAS, J.) (advocating the overruling of Griswold, Lawrence, and Obergefell). But how is it possible? The majority's only justification for its actions today is that the right to choose an abortion is not "deeply entrenched in history." According to the majority, it wasn't until Roe that people began to believe that abortion was covered by the Constitution's guarantee of liberty. At 32, ante. However, the bulk of the rights that they claim they are not interfering with may be considered to be similarly affected.

The majority might have written an opinion that was just as lengthy demonstrating, for instance, that up until the middle of the 20th century, "there was no grounding in American law for a constitutional right to receive [contraceptives]." at 15 ante. Thus, one of two possibilities must be true.

Either the majority is not really convinced by its own arguments. If it does, then any rights that don't date back to the middle of the 19th century are unstable. Either the majority's position is hypocritical, or more constitutional liberties are in jeopardy. One or the other applies.

One piece of evidence appears particularly relevant on that point: the majority's hasty decision to overrule this Court's precedents. The Latin word "stare decisis" refers to the idea that decisions made should stand unless there is a very strong cause to modify them.

It is a judicial modesty and humility ideology. In today's view, such attributes are not readily apparent. The majority has no justification for the changes it causes to the law and society. Women's perceptions of their options when an unintended pregnancy happens are shaped by Roe and Casey, which have been the law of the nation for decades.

Abortion has been a tool that women have used to structure their relationships and arrange their lives. In courts around the nation, the legal structure Roe and Casey created to reconcile the conflicting interests in this area has shown to be effective. No recent changes in the law or the facts have undermined or called into question previous precedents. In other words, nothing has changed.

In fact, the Court in Casey previously determined that all of it was accurate. A precedent concerning a precedent is Casey. It examined the identical justifications advanced here in favor of overturning Roe and determined that doing so was not necessary. Today, the Court takes a different tack for only one reason—that the Court's makeup has changed. By ensuring that rulings are "based in the law rather than in the inclinations of persons," stare decisis, as this Court has often said, "contributes to the real and apparent integrity of the judicial process." Vasquez v. Hillery, 474 U. S. 254, 265; Payne v. Tennessee, 501 U. S. 808, 827 (1991); (1986).

Today, personal preferences are what matter. The Court violates its duty to apply the law fairly and sincerely. We disagree.

We begin with Roe and Casey because of their close ties to a significant portion of this Court's earlier decisions. According to the bulk of accounts, Roe and Casey are exceptions: They had nowhere to go and nothing to come from, making it simple to excuse them under this country's fundamental framework. This is untrue.

Following a description of the choices, we go through how they are connected to—and in turn, lead to—other rights that give people autonomy over their bodies and their most private and intimate relationships. For obvious reasons, the majority does not want to discuss these issues; doing so would both enshrine Roe and Casey in this Court's precedents and make clear the vast ramifications of today's ruling. However, the truth won't go away that easily. Roe and Casey were ingrained in fundamental constitutional principles of individual freedom and the equal right of people to choose the course of their lives from the outset and much more so now. One may even argue that such legal ideas significantly contributed to the definition of what it means to be an American.

Because in our country, we do not think that a free people and a government that controls all personal decisions are compatible. Therefore, we do not put everything within "the grasp of majorities and [government] officials," as the majority of people urge nowadays. Barnette v. West Virginia Board of Education, 319 U. S. 624, 638 (1943). We support a Constitution that prohibits majority control in certain situations. We defend people's freedom to choose their own paths in life, especially women, even in the face of widespread resistance. At the very least, we once did.

A

Roe overturned a state statute that made abortion illegal unless it was necessary to save a woman's life more than 50 years ago. The Roe Court was aware that it was stepping on shaky and contentious ground. It recognized that many persons had "opposing perspectives" on abortion due to their "experiences," "values," and "religious upbringing" and beliefs. 410 U. S., at 116. By a majority of 7 to 2, the Court decided that in the early stages of pregnancy, the woman must make the contentious and contestable decision after consulting with her family and physicians.

The Court said that individual choice in "marriage, procreation, contraception, family relationships, and child raising and education" was protected by a long line of decisions "based in the Fourteenth Amendment's principle of personal liberty." Id., at 152-153 (citations omitted).

The Constitution must safeguard "a woman's choice whether or not to terminate her pregnancy," the Court said, for the same reasons. Id., at 153. The Court acknowledged the many ways having a child may change a woman's "life and destiny" as well as the lives of her family members. Ibid. A State could not trump all "rights of the pregnant woman" by "adopting one theory of life." Id., at 162.

But at the same time, the Court acknowledged the State's "legitimate interests[s]" in "controlling the abortion choice." Id., at 153. The Court cited "important interests," including "saving potential life," "maintaining medical standards," and "safeguarding [the] health," of the lady as being of special importance. Id., at 154. Those important governmental claims could not be eliminated by a "absolut[ist]" understanding of the woman's right. Ibid.

As a result, the Court found a balance based on the point in the pregnancy when the abortion would take place. The Court said that initially, a woman's decision must be respected, but eventually, "the state interests" take precedence. Id., at 155. Then it provided some benchmarks. The State has no right to intervene in a woman's choice to end her pregnancy during the first trimester of her pregnancy.

After that, the State may regulate to safeguard the unborn child's health, such as by requiring that abortion clinics and facilities adhere to safety standards. The State may also outlaw abortions once the baby reaches viability, or the time when it "has the possibility of meaningful existence outside the mother's womb," unless it's absolutely required to protect the woman's life or health. Id., at 163–164.

Between Roe and Casey, a period of 20 years, the Court explicitly reaffirmed Roe twice and applied it several times. The notion of stare decisis "demands respect in a society controlled by the rule of law," we said, acknowledging that "arguments [against Roe] continue to be advanced." Akron v. Akron Center for Reproductive Health, Inc., 462 U. S. 416, 419-420 (1983).

We further swore that "constitutional values cannot be permitted to succumb just because of disagreement with them" due to their "vitality." American College of Obstetricians and Gynecologists v. Thornburgh, 476 US 747, 759 (1986). As a result, the Court repeatedly upheld the fundamental principles Roe had established. Consider the following cases: Ohio v. Akron Center for Reproductive Health, 497 U.S. 502 (1990); Hodgson v. Minnesota, 497 U.S. 417 (1990); Simopoulos v. Virginia, 462 U.S. 506 (1983); Planned Parenthood Assn. of Kansas City, Mo., Inc. v. Ashcroft, 462 U.S. 476 (1983); H. L. v. (1976).

The Court then reexamined the situation in Casey and maintained Roe's fundamental principles once again. Casey is one of the Court's most significant precedents to date and is in large part a precedent regarding the concept of precedent. But we'll get to that part of the court's ruling later. The Court's thoughtful conclusion that "the core finding of Roe v. Wade should be kept and once again reaffirmed" relates to the substantive issue at hand. 505 U. S., at 846.

That conclusion included a strong affirmation of a woman's freedom to make her own decisions. Casey, like Roe, based this right on the promise of "liberty" in the Fourteenth Amendment. This principle extends to areas of behavior that the Constitution does not address directly. Despite this, the Court was "without a doubt correct" in upholding the right to marry "against governmental intervention." 505 U. S., at 847-848. Additionally, behavior that was not protected at the time of the Fourteenth Amendment is now included in the guarantee of liberty. Viewed at 848 in id.

Although it was not always so, the Court said that "it is accepted today that a State's ability to interfere with a person's most fundamental choices about family and parenting, as well as physical integrity, is limited by the Constitution." Id., at 849 (citations omitted); see also id., at 851, where it is stated that "personal choices related to marriage, procreation, contraception, [and] family ties" are protected by the constitution. This network of precedents safeguarding a person's most "personal decisions" was especially significant for the right to contraception. See id., at 852-853, or ibid. In such instances, the Court had acknowledged "the individual's right" to make the very important "choice whether to carry" a child. Id., at 851 (emphasis deleted). Casey concluded that the liberty clause also protects a woman's choice when she faces an unintended pregnancy. The choice she made about the abortion was crucial to her ability to choose the direction of her life. Viewed at 853, id.

The Court fully considered the variety of perspectives on abortion as well as the significance of numerous conflicting state interests in confirming the right Roe recognized. The Supreme Court noted that some Americans "consider [abortion] little short of an act of murder against innocent human life." 505 U. S., at 852. Additionally, as Roe itself had acknowledged, each State had a stake in "the safeguarding of potential life." 505 U. S., at 871 (plurality opinion). That interest, on the one hand, was inconclusive. The "moral and spiritual" issues raised by abortion could not be "resolved" by the State in "such a definitive way that a woman lacks all choice in the matter." Id., at 850 (majority opinion). When she would have preferred an early abortion, it could not make her endure the "pain" and "physical restrictions" of "car[ry[ing] a kid] to full term." Id., at 852.

However, the State has, as Roe had argued, a very strong interest in forbidding abortions in the latter stages of a pregnancy. Additionally, it had a constant desire to "ensure[that] the woman's decision is informed" and advocate for "choos[ing] childbirth over abortion." 505 U. S., at 878 (plurality opinion).

So Casey again established a balance, just slightly deviating from Roe's. It upheld Roe's "core holding," according to which the State may only prohibit abortions prior to viability. 505 U. S., at 860 (majority opinion). The viability line, in Casey's opinion, was "more feasible" than any other in designating the point at which the woman's interest in her liberty was superseded by a State's attempts to protect potential life. Id., at 870 (plurality opinion). A "second life" was then capable of having a "independent existence." Ibid. The lady lacked sufficient grounds to protest "the

State's involvement on [the growing child's] behalf" if she had not taken action at that point. Ibid.

At the same time, Casey determined that the Roe framework did not offer States enough power to control abortion before viability based on his 20 years of experience. In that time, Casey now made it apparent, the State might regulate in order to "promote [prenatal life]" in addition to protecting the woman's health. 505 U. S., at 873 (plurality opinion) (plurality opinion). In particular, the State might guarantee informed decision-making and make an effort to encourage births. Look at id., p. 877-878. However, the State was still not allowed to impede a woman seeking an abortion with a "undue burden" or "significant impediment." Id., at 878. Prior to becoming viable, the woman must "retain the ultimate power over her future and her body," in accordance with the constitutional "meaning of liberty." Id., at 869.

In view of the majority's argument that Roe and Casey, and we in defending them, are dismissive of a "State's interest in safeguarding fetal life," we make one basic remark regarding this approach. at 38, ante. Nothing could be more incorrect than such choices.

According to what was recently said, Roe and Casey cited strong state interests in that protection that were applicable at all stages of pregnancy and superseded the woman's right to liberty beyond viability. The Court permitted more limits on the right to an abortion than on other rights derived from the Fourteenth Amendment precisely because of the importance of those state interests. But Roe and Casey both understood that a woman's freedom and equality are also at stake, but the majority of people today do not. The existence of competing interests made the abortion debate challenging and called for a delicate balancing act

. The majority scorns such notion, accusing us of "repeatedly praising the 'balancing'" the two instances ultimately reached (note the scare quotes around the term "balance"). at 38, ante. "Balance" is a bad word to the majority since moderation is an alien idea. The majority does not believe that forced childbearing in any way affects a woman's rights to equality and freedom, hence it would be acceptable for States to outlaw abortion beginning at conception.

The Court of today, then, does not believe that a woman's sovereignty over her body and course in life has any constitutionally significant implications. Roe and Casey believed such viewpoint was biased and unwise. That, in a nutshell, is the main difference between the majority decision and our precedents. The constitutional system that has governed our country for the last 50 years acknowledged conflicting interests and worked to strike a balance between them. Our current constitutional system ignores the woman's interests and only acknowledges those of the State (or the Federal Government).

B

The adjustment is made by the majority in response to a single query: Was the reproductive right recognized in Roe and Casey present in "1868, the year the Fourteenth Amendment was ratified"? At 23 ante. The answer, according to the majority (and on this point, we are all in agreement), is no. In 1868, there was no idea that the Fourteenth Amendment guaranteed a national right to stop a pregnancy.

Naturally, the prevailing view also makes reference to some previous and later history. It dates back to the 13th (the 13th!) century on one side of 1868. look at ante, at 17. But that ultimately proves to be pointless. First, even for the majority, it is unclear what importance such ancient history should have. Bruen, 597 U. S. (2022), New York State Rifle & Pistol Assn., Inc. v. (slip op., at 26) "Historical evidence that precedes [ratification] may not provide light on the breadth of the right." The majority would undoubtedly claim that the opinions of the Fourteenth Amendment's ratifiers are the sole relevant ones if early history had clearly favored abortion rights.

Visit ibid. Except in cases when ancient "law survived to become our Founders' law," it is "best not to delve too far back into antiquity." Second, early legislation does in fact favor abortion rights to some extent, which is uncomfortable for the majority. Before the baby started moving in the womb, or before "quickening," common-law authorities did not consider abortion to be a crime. Additionally, common law was followed in early American law. 3 Since Roe and Casey treated early and late abortions differently, the criminal law of that era might be said to be fairly consistent with those two cases. So it is better to advance time. The majority sometimes points out that several States had abortion restrictions up to the Roe decision on the opposite side of 1868. Ante, pp. 24, 36 Although it is practical for the majority, that is only window decoration.

"Post-ratification approval or acceptance of measures that are incongruous with the original meaning of the constitutional language plainly cannot override or modify that text," the same majority (plus one) just said. 597 U. S., at - New York State Rifle & Pistol Assn., Inc. (slip op., at 27–28). The majority would assert (again) that only the opinions of the ratifiers are relevant if the pre-Roe relaxation of abortion restrictions had taken place more swiftly and broadly in the 20th century.

The fundamental legal tenet of the majority is that we in the twenty-first century must interpret the Fourteenth Amendment in the same way that its ratifiers did. And indeed, it is what the majority reiterates again and time again. The most significant historical fact is how the States controlled abortion at the time the Fourteenth Amendment was written, as stated in the ante at 47; moreover, see the ante at 5, 16, and n. 24, 23, 25, 28. We cannot understand something as essential to freedom if the ratifiers did not. Or, to be more precise: If those individuals did not recognize reproductive rights as a component of the guarantee of liberty granted by the Fourteenth Amendment, then such rights do not exist.

First, take notice of the error in the previous statement. The "people" who ratified the Fourteenth Amendment were referred to there as follows: What rights, in their minds, did the "people" have at the time? Of course, the Fourteenth Amendment was not ratified by the "people." Guys did. That the ratifiers were not fully aware of the significance of reproductive rights for women's freedom or for their ability to engage as equal citizens of our country may not come as a huge surprise. In fact, neither the ratifiers of the original Constitution in 1788 nor those of the 1868 amendment understood women to be full members of the society covered by the term "We the People."

The first generation of American feminists were expressly advised not to seek constitutional protections in 1868, naturally by males. (Women would not even be granted the right to vote for another 50 years.) Yes, the majority of women in 1868 also had a condensed understanding of their rights.

Most women could not have imagined having that level of autonomy at that time, just as most men could not have imagined granting women control over their bodies. But it doesn't change the essential premise in any way. Women were not seen as equals or given the same rights as males by those who drafted the original Constitution and the Fourteenth Amendment. Women are relegated to second-class citizenship when the majority asserts that we must interpret our founding document as it was understood at the time of ratification (albeit we may also compare it to the Dark Ages).

As will become apparent, Casey was aware of this. See below, pages 23–24. It remembered with regret a ruling this Court made barely five years after the Fourteenth Amendment was ratified, endorsing a State's choice to refuse a woman a law license and implying that a woman had no other legal standing save her husband. Bradwell v. State, 16 Wall. 130 (1873), is cited in the majority decision in 505 U.S. at 896 and 897. Casey said that there was a period when "men and women alike" were not protected by the Constitution. 505 U. S., at 896. However, times had evolved. Constitutional law has evolved along with the role of women in society. It was "no longer compatible with our view" of the Constitution to reduce women to second-class citizens or members of the family. Id., at 897. The Constitution now "protects all persons, male or female," against "the misuse of governmental authority" or "unjustified state involvement." Id., at 896, 898.

So how is it that, as Casey pointed out, our Constitution today, read as it was in 1868, gives women rights? Why does our Constitution need greater judicial scrutiny of discrimination against them? How is it that women may choose for themselves whether and when to have children since our Constitution, under the liberty clause of the Fourteenth Amendment, allows access to contraception (which was also not legally protected in 1868)? How is it that up until recently, the same constitutional provision guaranteed a woman's freedom to terminate a pregnancy early if contraception proved ineffective?

The majority's narrow interpretation of how to interpret our Constitution has been rejected by this Court, which is why. The Founders "understood they were crafting a constitution meant to adapt to ever-changing conditions across centuries," as we previously said in a piece.

Noel Canning v. NLRB, 573 U.S. 513, 533-534 (2014). Or, in the words of the late Chief Justice John Marshall, our Constitution must, if at all, adapt to a future that is "seen dimly" since it is "designed to survive for millennia to come." Maryland v. McCulloch (4 Wheat. 316, 415 (1819). In fact, it is the reason behind the way our Constitution is drafted.

The Framers recognized that the world was changing both in 1788 and in 1868. Therefore, they did not define rights in terms of the particular practices that were in use at the time. Instead, in order to allow for future change in their scope and significance, the Framers defined rights in generic terms. And this Court has accepted the Framers' invitation throughout our history. By adapting the Framers' concepts to modern circumstances and social understandings, it has remained loyal to their original intent.

This kind of thinking has never been more common than when interpreting the Fourteenth Amendment's lofty but ambiguous promises of "liberty" and "equality" for everyone. And nowhere has that strategy given this nation and the Court more reasons to be proud. Think about an illustration Obergefell gave a few years ago.

The Court there dealt with a claim that the Fourteenth Amendment "must be construed in a very restricted fashion, with essential reference to certain historical practices"—exactly the position today's majority holds. This argument was predicated on Washington v. Glucksberg, 521 U. S. 702 (1997). 671 in Obergefell, 576 U.S. And the Court expressly disapproved of such viewpoint. The Court considered the implications of the proposed, historically constrained approach for interracial marriage while doing this. Visit ibid. The ratifiers of the Fourteenth Amendment disagreed that it granted black and white people the freedom to marry. Contrarily, current practice saw such conduct as being just as unprotected as abortion.

The Court nonetheless interpreted the Fourteenth Amendment to recognize the Lovings' union in Loving v. Virginia, 388 U. S. 1 (1967). If, as Obergefell put it, "rights were defined by who exercised them in the past, then received practices might serve as their own continuous justification"—even when they go against "liberty" and "equality" as later and more generally understood—received practices could be justified. 576 U. S., at 671. The initial understanding of what such rights provide or how they operate is not permanently preserved by the Constitution.

Nothing necessarily follows from it. The majority wants people to believe that there are only two options: either accept the Fourteenth Amendment's original provisions and none else, or submit to judges' "own impassioned opinions," which are unsupported by the law, regarding the "liberty that Americans should enjoy." at 14 ante. At least, it's the message that the majority will sometimes try to express. Other times, the majority (or rather, most of it) tries to reassure the public that it has no intentions of taking away rights (like the right to contraception), which only emerged in the second half of the 20th century; in other words, that it is content to pick and choose in accordance with personal preferences.

However, see ante, at 3 (KAVANAUGH, J. concurring); see ante, at 32, 66, 71–72; and ante, at 10. (THOMAS, J., concurring). But it is a subject for a later discussion. See below, pages 24-29. Currently, our argument is distinct: It is the ability to adapt how liberty and equality are applied while maintaining a firm foundation in constitutional precepts, constitutional precedents, and constitutional history. When explaining why he would have overturned a State's restriction on the use of contraceptives, Justice Harlan II spoke about how to achieve the correct balance. Judges are not "allowed to travel where unguided conjecture could lead them," according to him. 367 U. S. 497, 542 (1961) Poe v. Ullman (dissenting opinion). However, they must also understand that this nation's constitutional "tradition" cannot be fully reflected in a single instance. Ibid.

Instead, the length of our history and subsequent court precedents—each looking to the last and attempting to apply the Constitution's most basic provisions to new circumstances—give it depth. Because of this, Americans have the freedom to wed people of different races, to use Obergefell's example once again. To return to Justice Harlan's argument, this is the reason why people in America have the freedom to utilize contraceptives so they may decide for themselves whether or not to have children.

That is everything Casey realized. Casey flatly criticized the strategy of the ruling majority. The boundaries of the substantive realm of liberty that the Fourteenth Amendment protects are not "marked[]" by the particular practices of States at the time of the Fourteenth Amendment's passage, according to Casey. 505 U. S., at 848.

The majority's current position that doing differently "would be incongruous with our law." Id., at 847. Why? Because the Court repeatedly "vindicated [the] principle" that, regardless of the sentiment in 1868, "there is a realm of personal liberty which the government may not enter"—especially in relation to "bodily integrity" and "family life"—"there is a realm of personal liberty which the government may not enter." Id., at 847, 849, 851. Casey went into great depth on the court's cases involving contraception. Id. at 848, 849, and 851, and 853 It mentioned rulings defending the freedom to marry, even to someone of a different race. See id., at 847-848 ("Interracial marriage was outlawed in the majority of States throughout the 19th century, but the Court was without a doubt right in determining it to be an element of liberty protected against governmental intervention").

Casey was only able to come to one conclusion after studying decades upon decades of constitutional law: Whatever the case may have been back in 1868, "[i]t is established today, as it was when the Court heard arguments in Roe v. Wade, that the Constitution establishes restrictions on a State's ability to interfere with a person's most fundamental choices about family and parenting," according to the Supreme Court. Id., at 849.

Up to the Court's participation in this case, the conclusion was still valid. The Constitution restricts a State's ability to exert control over a person's body and most private decisions. This was established in the Roe v. Wade, Casey v. Washington, and yesterday cases. The freedom to choose was acknowledged by Roe and reiterated by Casey as a result of several cases upholding that concept; Roe and Casey then backed the insertion of new safeguards for close and family relationships. Surprisingly nothing is being said about such precedents by the majority. It literally lists them out in a single paragraph and makes the implication that they are unrelated to one another or the right to end an unplanned pregnancy.

See supra, at 31–32 (arguing that by acknowledging a connection between them as addressing components of human autonomy, it would inescapably "license basic rights" to prostitution and illicit drug use). But it is just false. Our constitutional law, and thus, our lives, are intertwined with the court's rulings on physical autonomy, sexual and family relationships, and reproduction. particularly in the lives of women, where they protect the freedom to self-determination.

And deleting that right is not adopting a "neutral" stance, as JUSTICE KAVANAUGH seeks to claim, we must state before going on to discuss our precedents. at, 2-3, 5, 7, 11–12, and ante (concurring opinion). He contends that the only way to maintain objectivity is to let the States decide how to handle the abortion debate. But if the Court permitted New York and California to impose whatever gun restrictions they choose, would he still claim that it is acting "scrupulously neutrally"?

If the Court permitted certain States to utilize unanimous juries but not others, why? Ante, at 3. What if the Court had instructed the States to make their own decisions on limits on church attendance? We could — and will — continue. Suppose JUSTICE KAVANAUGH were to assert that the rights we just named are more textually or historically rooted than the freedom to choose, in accordance with the majority position. So what about the right to abortion or same-sex unions?

Would the Court's elimination of such rights be "scrupulously neutral" as well? All of these instances serve to illustrate the argument that when the Court defers to the States on all matters pertaining to rights, it is not acting "neutrally." Instead, the Court defends the right against all adversaries in an impartial manner. In this instance, the Court is not being "scrupulously impartial" when it eliminates a privilege that women have possessed for 50 years. Instead, it is siding with states (like Mississippi) that seek to restrict women from exercising their right.

JUSTICE KAVANAUGH cannot distort that point by using the language of fairness. His stance is what it is: a brook-no-compromise denial of the woman's ability to make her own decisions beginning on the first day of her pregnancy. And as we'll see in a moment, this Court has long held the opinion that women do, in fact, have the right to make the most intimate and significant choices about their bodies and their lives, regardless of the political climate in 1868.

the legal precedent set by this Court defending "bodily integrity." 849 in Casey, 505 U.S. No right "is regarded more sacrosanct, or is more diligently guarded," in the words of this Court, "than the right of every individual to the ownership and control of his own person." 141 U.S. 250, 251 (1891) and Cruzan v. Director, Mo. Dept. of Health, 497 U.S. 261, 269 are examples of Union Pacific R. Co. v. Botsford cases (1990) Each adult "has a right to choose what should be done with his own body," according to this. Or, to put it more succinctly: Everyone—women included—owns their own bodies.

As a result, the Court has limited the government's ability to influence a person's medical choices or force her to have certain surgeries or treatments. See, for instance,

Winston v. Lee (forced surgery), 470 U.S. 753, 766-767 (1985); Rochin v. California (forced stomach pumping), 342 U.S. 165, 166, 173-174 (1952); and Washington v. Harper, 494 U.S. 210, 229, 236 (1990). (forced administration of antipsychotic drugs).

505 U.S. at 857, Casey acknowledged the "doctrinal kinship" between those decisions and Roe. And that factual similarity gives rise to that theological affinity. Few bodily invasions are worse than making a woman carry her pregnancy to term and give birth. Every woman will go through a variety of bodily changes, medical procedures, including possible cesarean sections, and other risks. For instance, an American woman has a 14-fold greater risk of dying from bringing a pregnancy to term than from getting an abortion.

See Hellerstedt v. Whole Woman's Health, 579 U. S. 582, 618. (2016). The fact that women willingly subject themselves to such costs and risks does not decrease the extent to which a State interferes with a woman's body when it forces her to carry a pregnancy to term. And as Roe acknowledged, some women need abortions for medical reasons to protect themselves. Check out 410 U.S. at 153. The majority is silent on the question of whether a State may forbid a woman from getting an abortion when she and her doctor have concluded it is a necessary medical treatment, which is concerning in and of itself.

So too do Roe and Casey perfectly fit into a long series of judgments shielding a plethora of private decisions concerning family concerns, child raising, personal relationships, and reproduction from governmental meddling. See Roe, 410 U.S. at 152-153; Casey, 505 U.S. at 851, 857; and ante, at 31–32. (listing the myriad decisions of this kind that Casey relied on).

These cases defend specific decisions including who to marry, with whom to have sex, with whom to live, how to raise children, and most importantly, whether and when to have children. The Court has argued in a number of instances that such decisions—which are "the most private and personal" that a person can make—reflect essential facets of the self and establish the very "attributes of personality." 505 U.S. at 851, Casey. And they unavoidably influence the character and direction of a person's life in the future (and often the lives of those closest to her). The Court ruled that the person, not the government, has the right to make such decisions. That is the fundamental need for liberty.

This Court has emphasized several times that liberty may demand it even though people in 1868 would not have understood the claim because they would not have regarded the individual making it as an equal member of the society. The area of liberty that is protected has grown throughout the course of our history, embracing those who were previously shut out.

In this manner, liberty and equality, which are fundamental American principles, go hand in hand rather than being in the hermetically walled compartments that the majority presents. Compare ante, at 10-11, with Obergefell, 576 U. S., at 672–675. As a result, before Roe and Casey, the Court enlarged in subsequent instances who may assert the right to marry, even if their relationships would not have been covered by the law at the time.

See, for instance, Loving, 388 U. S. 1, which dealt with interracial couples, Turner v. Safley, 482 U. S. 78 (1987), which dealt with inmates, and Stanley v. Illinois, 405 U. S. 645, 651-652 (1972), which provided protection under the constitution to unconventional "family unit[s]". Naturally, the Court proceeded in that spirit after Roe and Casey. The Court determined that the Fourteenth Amendment also gave same-sex couples the freedom to be married after making a crucial decision to hold that the Amendment protected same-sex intimacy. See Obergefell, 576 U.S. 644; Lawrence, 539 U.S. 558. According to the Court, "[h]istory and tradition," particularly as shown in the development of our precedent, "guide and discipline [the] investigation" while debating that issue. Id., at 664. However, the feelings of 1868 do not, and cannot, "control the present" on their own. Ibid.

Casey saw the need of include a group that had hitherto been excluded in the constitutionally guaranteed realm of liberty. The Court recognized at the time, unlike the majority now, that males did not consider women as full and equal citizens when they adopted the Fourteenth Amendment and drafted the state laws of the day. Observe supra, p. In those days, a woman "had no legal existence independent from her husband," according to Casey. 505 U. S., at 897. Women were not given "complete and autonomous legal position under the Constitution," just as "the heart of the home and family life." Ibid.

However, it was no longer valid: The State could no longer cling to the prevailing "image of the woman's function" from the past. Id., at 852. Casey also knew that reproductive rights were inextricably linked to equal citizenship. The freedom of women to regulate their reproductive lives has made it easier for them to participate equally in all facets of national life, including its economic, social, political, and legal dimensions. Id., at 856. Women would not be able to control their lives and how they would contribute to society in the same way men could if they were unable to chose whether and when to have children.

Casey made it apparent that Roe closely followed precedents regarding contraception because of this. The Court had determined in three decisions that the Fourteenth Amendment's protection of liberty included the freedom to use and have access to contraception. See, for example, Griswold (381 U.S. 479); Eisenstadt (405 U.S. 438); and Carey v. Population Services International (431 U.S. 678). (1977).

The right "to be free from unjustified state intervention into things so profoundly affecting a person as the choice whether to carry or beget a child" was unavoidably guaranteed by that provision, we reasoned. See Carey, 431 U.S. at 684–685, and Eisenstadt, 405 U.S. at 453.

In Casey's opinion, Roe and the choice to have an abortion are similar in important ways. 505 U. S., at 852. The Court said that "reasonable individuals" may also be against contraception. In fact, they might think that "certain types of contraception" likewise raise issues with "potential life." Id., at 853, 859. However, a woman's freedom to regulate her own body and to decide whether to have—and likely raise—a child could not always be overruled by the opinions of others. Because contraception or abortion are illegal when an unwanted pregnancy is involved, "the liberty of the woman is at risk in a degree unique to the human situation." Id., at 852. No State could decide to "definitively" answer the moral issues in a manner that robs a woman of her freedom of choice. Id., at 850.

The majority assures everyone not to worry in the face of all these linkages between Roe/Casey and court rulings recognizing additional fundamental rights. It claims that it may elegantly remove the right to make one's own decisions from the constitutional framework without compromising any related rights. (Consider someone telling you that the Jenga tower won't really fall.)

The majority begins by stating that today's judgment "does not weaken" in any manner the rulings mentioned by Roe and Casey that deal with "marriage, procreation, contraception, [and] family connections." Casey, 505 U. S. at 851, and Ante at 32. Be aware that the rights to same-sex marriage and intimacy, which are in part founded on Roe and Casey, are not covered by this first guarantee. see above, p. 23.

However, in its subsequent try, the majority also adds those: "Nothing in this decision should be interpreted to call into question precedents not pertaining to abortion." See ante, pages 71–72, and ante, at 66.

The majority argues that this right is special since "abortion ends life or prospective life." See ante, at 32, 71–72, and ante, at 66 (internal quotation marks omitted). So, according to the majority, today's judgment is "a limited railroad ticket, valid for this day and train only." Smith v. Allwright (1944), 321 U. S. 649, 669 (Roberts, J., dissenting). Should the audience for these protests, which are too often repeated, be properly satiated? No, we believe.

The concurrence of JUSTICE THOMAS, which makes it apparent that he disagrees with the program, is the first issue with the majority's statement. JUSTICE THOMAS notes that when he says that nothing in today's ruling calls into question non-abortion precedents, he simply means that they are not in question in this particular case. "This case does not afford the opportunity to reject" those precedents, according to ante, at 7.

But when they are, he lets us know what he intends to do. We should reevaluate all of this Court's substantive due process decisions, including Griswold, Lawrence, and Obergefell, he argues, in future instances. See also above, at 25, and n. 6;

ante, at 3. And after reevaluating them? Then "we have a responsibility" to "overrul[e]" these blatantly incorrect judgments. at 3 ante. Therefore, at least one Justice intends to utilize today's decision's ticket over and over again.

In today's judgement, the assurance is nonetheless ineffective even after putting the concurrence to one side. At least if the majority really believes that the legal status of abortion in the 19th century is the only justification for reversing Roe and Casey. The state's interest in preserving fetal life does not factor into the majority's argument, with the exception of the passages mentioned above.

The majority, on the other hand, takes satisfaction in not having an opinion "regarding the status of the fetus." See ante, at 32 (aligning with Roe and Casey's position of not judging whether life or prospective life is involved); ante, at 38–39. Ante, at 65. (similar).

Instead—and solely—whether a woman's choice to stop a pregnancy contains any Fourteenth Amendment liberty interest is what drives the majority's departure from Roe and Casey (against which Roe and Casey balanced the state interest in preserving fetal life).

The majority contends that no liberty interest exists because, and only because, in the 19th century, the law did not provide protection for a woman's right to choose. But here's the catch: Additionally, a vast array of other items were not protected by the law back then and would not be for years.

It did not safeguard the same-sex marriage and intimate relations rights established in Lawrence and Obergefell. The freedom to marry outside of one's race, as acknowledged in Loving, was not protected. It did not defend the Griswold-recognized right to take contraception. Additionally, it did not defend the prohibition on forced sterilization established in Skinner v. Oklahoma ex rel. Williamson, 316 U.S. 535 (1942).

Therefore, regardless of the specific state interests involved, all those judgements were incorrect and all those subjects should belong to the States if the majority is correct in its legal view. And if that is the case, it is incomprehensible (both logically and morally) how the majority can claim that their position today does not jeopardize or even "undermine" any other fundamental rights. At 32, ante.

It also doesn't help to just accept the majority's word. Assume that the majority is honest when they declare that it will only go so far and stop, for whatever reason. Honor of a scout. However, the future will determine how important today's view will be. And law often develops without taking into account the initial goals; rather than allowing difficult-to-explain lines, it frequently follows where logic leads. This is one way that rights may grow.

Justice Scalia said in his Lawrence dissent that he could not find solace in the Court's declaration that a ruling recognizing the right to same-sex intimacy did "not include" same-sex marriage. 539 U. S., at 604. "Only if one entertains the assumption that principle and logic have nothing to do with the judgments of this Court," he said, "could it be true." Id., at 605. As a matter of prophesy, the disagreement gets a point. Principle and logic are both two-way ratchets. Regardless of what the majority of today would claim, one thing actually does lead to another, therefore rights might contract in the same manner and for the same reason. We really hope that today's ruling prevents that from happening. We hope that we won't end up in the book of prophets with Justice Scalia. But we fail to see how anybody could be sure that this view is the last one of its sort.

As a last thought on this subject, think about contraception. Of course, the term is not used in the Constitution. Additionally, historically speaking, the majority's preferred form of contraception does not exist. Contrarily, restrictions on the selling of contraceptive devices were common in American law during the decades after the Civil War. Again, it seems that there are two options. See above, pp. 5, 26–27. If the majority is sincere about its historical perspective, then Griswold and its descendants are also in danger. What led to today's choice, or if it's not a severe issue? If we were to hazard a prediction, we would say there is little chance this Court would approve prohibitions on contraception. But once again, the future will determine how important today's view will be. The current viewpoint will, at the very least, intensify the struggle to move morally charged topics like contraception out of the Fourteenth Amendment and into state legislatures.

Anyway, today's choice is disastrous enough on its own. The majority's determination to duplicate every definition of liberty held in 1868 in 2022 has very little to support it in terms of constitutional procedure. Our law has operated differently for decades and decades in this area of constitutional law, as it does in most others. Fundamental constitutional concepts, the whole of the nation's history and traditions, and the gradual development of the Court's precedents have all been taken into consideration. It is orderly yet not rigid. It is based on collective judgements rather than simply the opinions of one long-ago generation of men (who themselves believed, and drafted the Constitution to reflect, that the world progresses). And instead of maintaining the boundaries of that earlier discourse, it does so by including those who were left out.

The majority's position contains all the methodological faults that its constitutional essence would imply. Because of laws that denied women any choice over their bodies in 1868, most people are in favor of states doing the same thing now. The majority believes that States may once again enact laws that restrict women's ability to choose their own lives since earlier laws did so. The government may once again enforce that mandate since in 1868 it was legal to inform a pregnant woman that her only option was to have a child, even in the early stages of her pregnancy.

The verdict made today deprives women of autonomy over a moral problem that even the majority acknowledges is debatable and contestable. No matter the situation or the pain it would do to her and her family, she is compelled to carry out the State's wishes. In terms of the Fourteenth Amendment, it robs her of her freedom. We disagree even before we reach stare decisis.

II The majority abandons stare decisis, a fundamental precept of the rule of law, by overturning Roe, Casey, and more than 20 rulings that reaffirmed or applied the constitutional right to abortion. To "stand by decisions made" is to "stare decisis." 1696 Black's Law Dictionary (11th ed. 2019).

It was the "settled norm to follow prior precedents," according to Blackstone. Stare decisis "promotes the evenhanded, predictable, and consistent evolution of legal principles," according to 1 Blackstone 69. 827 in Payne, 501 U.S. It keeps things stable so that individuals may live their lives according to the law. The Legal Process: Basic Problems in the Making and Application of Law, by H. Hart and A. Sacks, 568–569 (1994).

By ensuring that judgments "are rooted on the law rather than in the preferences of people," stare decisis also "contributes to the integrity of our constitutional form of governance." 474 U.S. at 265, Vasquez. It "avoid[s] an arbitrary discretion in the courts," as Hamilton put it. Page 529 of The Federalist No. 78 (J. Cooke, 1961 ed) (A. Hamilton). Additionally, it "maintains the scale of justice equal and constant, and not likely to shift with every new judge's view," as Blackstone said before him. Blackstone, #1 69. Our legal system's "beauty" lies in the fact that it "gives primacy to precedent rather than jurists." Departure From Precedent by H. Humble, 19 Michigan Law Review 608, 614 (1921).

According to legend, Chief Justice John Marshall took the oath of office while wearing a simple black robe. That deed embodied an American custom. Law is not made by judges' personal preferences; rather, it is spoken by them.

This implies that without a "special rationale," the Court cannot reverse a decision—even one that is constitutional. United States v. Gamble, 587 U. S. (2019) (slip op., at 11). Stare decisis is obviously not a "inexorable edict"; there are instances when it is permissible to overturn a previous ruling. Callahan v. Pearson, 555 U. S. 223, 233 (2009). The Court must, however, have a strong justification for doing so in addition to the conviction "that the precedent was improperly decided." Erica P. John Fund, Inc. v. Halliburton Co., 573 U. S. 258, 266 (2014). "It is not enough that we would determine a case differently today than we did before," the author writes. Marvel Entertainment, LLC v. Kimble, 576 U. S. 446, 455 (2015).

The majority now claims that Roe and Casey should be overruled and cites around 30 of our decisions as precedent-busting examples. However, none do, as is shown in more detail below and in the Appendix. See below, pages 61–66. Some precedents were only partly changed or clarified by the Court.

In the remaining cases, the Court relied on one or more of the established stare decisis criteria to make its decision. The Court determined, for instance, that (1) a change in legal theory weakened or rendered the previous judgment outdated; (2) a change in the facts had the same effect; or (3) there was no need to rely on the earlier decision since it was issued less than ten years before. (While it is true that we insist on a test of altered law or fact alone in the majority of circumstances, this is incorrect. Refer to ante, at 69.) None of those circumstances exist here: Nothing, especially no substantial legal or factual change, warrants changing a half-century of established legislation that gives women authority over their reproductive life. First of all, Roe and Casey were accurate for all the reasons we have stated.

According to our Fourteenth Amendment precedents, the Court preserved women's equality and liberty by ruling that a State may not "resolve" the abortion dispute "in such a definite fashion that a woman lacks any choice in the matter." 505 U. S. Casey, at 850. Contrary to popular belief, the 19th century's legalization of abortion docs not make such choices any less valid.

Furthermore, the majority's recurrent claim that the "authority to address" a hotly debated subject is being "usurped" by state legislators does not assist it on this case's most important point. See ante, at 1, and ante, at 44. In other words, the purpose of a right is to protect individual behavior "from the vagaries of political dispute, to place it beyond the reach of majorities and officials and to establish it as legal principles to be implemented by courts." 319 U.S. at 638 for

Barnette; see also ante, at 7. A right is not subject to the will of the people, however controversial.

In any case, the remaining "principles of stare decisis weigh strongly against overruling" Roe and Casey. "Whether or not we... agree" with a previous decision is the beginning, not the conclusion, of our examination. United States v. Dickerson, 530 U. S. 428, 443 (2000).

In one of the most significant decisions about precedent from this Court, Casey itself adopted those concepts. Casey came to the only conclusion that was feasible after evaluating the conventional stare decisis factors: stare decisis is strongly at work here. It continues to. The requirements Roe and Casey outlined are entirely doable. The two rulings have not been undermined by changes in the law or the facts. And millions of American women have depended on their freedom to make their own decisions and still do. Therefore, the majority does not have a specific defense for the damage it creates under classic stare decisis standards.

In fact, the majority is on the verge of agreeing with that statement. The majority seldom cites any developments in the law or in the truth since Roe and Casey. It implies that the two rulings are difficult for courts to apply, but it is unable to substantiate this claim.

The majority claims that in the end, all it has to say to overturn stare decisis is that it thinks Roe and Casey are "egregiously erroneous." At 70, ante. That rule might also mean the demise of any precedent that the current Court disagrees with by a slim majority. How then can that strategy avoid the "scale of justice" "wavering[ing] with every new judge's opinion"? Blackstone 69, 1 There isn't. It makes drastic change too simple and quick, relying only on the fresh perspectives of new judges. Roe and Casey were overridden by the majority for one and only one reason: it has always hated them and now has the votes to throw them out. The rule of law is therefore replaced by a rule by judges by the majority.

A

Contrary to what the majority believes, Casey's "undue burden" threshold is not impractical. Its main concern is whether a State has put a "substantial impediment" in the way of a woman seeking an abortion. This is "the type of enquiry that courts across a number of situations are accustomed with." Russo, 591 U. S. (2020) (slip op., at 6) June Medical Services L. L. C. (ROBERTS, C. J., concurring in judgment). Furthermore, it hasn't caused any more application conflicts than many other standards that this Court and others unhesitatingly follow every day.

In the law and especially in constitutional adjudication, general principles, such as the excessive burden norm, are pervasive. This Court often creates adaptable standards that may be used case-by-case to a variety of unpredictable scenarios when called upon to give justice to the Constitution's broad ideals.

"No court putting down a broad rule can possibly anticipate the different situations" in which it must apply, according to Dickerson, 530 U.S. at 441 The Court, for instance, inquires into burdens that are excessive or significant on interstate trade, voting, and expression. Bennett v. Arizona Free Enterprise Club's Freedom Club PAC, 564 U.S. 721, 748 (2011); Burdick v. Takushi, 504 U.S. 428, 433-434 (1992); and Pike v. Bruce Church, Inc., 397 U.S. 137, 142 (2011) are a few examples (1970). It follows the same Casey unreasonable burden standard. The "rule of reason" in antitrust law or the "arbitrary and capricious" norm for agency decision-making are two examples of generic criteria that courts often use in various legal contexts. United States v. Standard Oil Co. of New Jersey, 221 U.S. 1, 62 (1911); Motor Vehicle Manufacturers Association of the United States, Inc. v. State Farm Mut. Automobile Insurance Co., 463 U.S. 29, 42-43 (1983). In many situations, practicing law simply entails applying broad rules to specific situations.

Furthermore, the "undue burden" criteria has not resulted in any particular problems. Naturally, it has led to some dissent among the justices. That much "is to be anticipated in the application of any legal norm which must accommodate life's complexity," Casey knew it would happen. 505 U. S., at 878 (plurality opinion). Which is to say: In the application of any legal norm, that much is to be anticipated.

However, the majority greatly exaggerates the differences in how judges apply the criteria. We effectively count two. THE CHIEF JUSTICE differed with the June Medical majority of Justices over whether Casey required for balancing the advantages and disadvantages of an abortion law. See ante, at 59, 60, and n. 53; 591 U.S., at ___ -___ (slip op., at 6-7).

We both believe that the June Medical distinction exists, but it is not one that, even if it were to ever matter, would significantly alter the outcome of the majority of instances (as it did not in June Medical).

In terms of lower courts, there is now a one-year-old, one-to-one Circuit split about how the undue hardship requirement applies to state laws that prohibit abortions for specific grounds, such as fetal abnormalities. Voir ante, p. 61, and n.

As far as what we can see, that's about all. That is not a lot, either. Because we are aware that some disagreement is unavoidably a feature of our legal system, this Court seldom even grants certiorari on one-year-old, one-to-one Circuit divides. An ancient proverb that may be applicable in this situation is that "not one or even a couple of swallows can make the majority's summer."

Anyone worried about applicability need to take the majority's replacement norm into account. An abortion-related legislation "must be retained if there is a logical basis on which the legislature may have assumed that it would serve legitimate state objectives," according to the majority. At 77, Ante.

The majority also mentions concerns like "respect for and preservation of unborn life," "protection of mother health," "abolition of certain "medical treatments," "mitigation of fetal discomfort," among other things. At 78, ante. This Court will undoubtedly be confronted with important questions concerning how that test applies. When an abortion is required to save a woman's life or health, must a state legislation permit it? And if so, when specifically? A woman's life may only be put in so much danger before the Fourteenth Amendment's protection of life takes effect. Is it sufficient if a patient with pulmonary hypertension has a 30- to 50-percent chance of dying while still pregnant?

How much disease or harm may the State force her to endure, short of death, while yet upholding the protections of liberty and equality provided by the Amendment? The application of abortion rules to medical treatment, which the majority of people consider as being quite distinct from abortion, may also raise issues for the Court.

The morning after pill, what about it? IUDs? What is in vitro fertilization? How about the treatment of miscarriages by the use of medicines or dilation and evacuation? For further information, see generally L. Harris, Navigating Loss of Abortion Services: A Large Academic Medical Center Prepares for Roe v. Wade's Reversal, 386 New England J. Med. 2061. (2022).

Finally, the majority's decision today raises several issues about interstate conflicts. 123 Colorado Law Review, The New Abortion Battleground, D. Cohen, G. Donley, & R. Rebouché, supra, at 3.

Can a State forbid women from leaving its borders to have an abortion there? Can a state outlaw promoting abortions performed beyond its borders or assisting women in finding such providers? Can a State obstruct the delivery of medications for medication abortions?

The decision of today will raise a number of new constitutional issues since the Constitution guarantees protection for interstate trade, free expression, and travel. The majority positions the Court at the epicenter of the next "interjurisdictional abortion conflicts," far from removing the Court from the abortion debate. Id., at (draft, at 1). (draft, at 1).

In other words, the majority does not shield judges from burdensome tests or remove them from the fray of debate. Instead, it abandons a tried-and-true norm in favor of something new that is almost certainly far more difficult. The majority critiques Roe and Casey for addressing contentious problems including moral and philosophical ones, yet this drives the Court to go even further into them.

B

The Court has nearly always cited significant legal or factual developments eroding a decision's initial legal or factual foundation when overturning constitutional precedent.

This may be seen by looking at the Appendix to this disagreement. See below, pages 61–66. This Court previously said that the majority of "successful proponent[s] of overruling precedent" have "borne the difficult burden of convincing the Court that developments in society or in the law mandate that the ideals supported by stare decisis surrender in favor of a larger purpose." At 266 in Vasquez, 474 U.S. Of the two primary cases the majority cites, West Coast Hotel Co. v. Parrish and Brown v. Board of Education, 347 U.S. 483 (1954) and 300 U.S. 379, it is undeniable that this is the case (1937). But that is not the case now.

The majority does not actually depend on "contemporary advances," while nodding to some of the points others have made about them since they can probably understand how tenuous they are. See ante at 34 for further information. The majority barely mentions the ongoing abortion debate. At 70–71, see the ante.

However, it must understand that the conflict over abortion is not a new issue, but rather one that has persisted for years. (And as we shall explore in more detail later, the existence of that ongoing disagreement gives us more justification to uphold current precedent than to throw it out.) See below, pages 55–57.) In the end, the majority radically reshapes the law without providing any evidence that anything material has changed to support their justification. 43 in the ante.

The legal changes that followed only strengthened Roe and Casey. All of the rulings mentioned by Roe and Casey, rulings that uphold an individual's constitutional freedom to make her own decisions regarding "intimate relationships, the family," and contraception, have been upheld by the Court. 857 in Casey, 505 U.S.

Roe and Casey laid the legal groundwork for later rulings defending these very personal decisions.

As was previously said, the Court used Casey in order to rule that same-sex intimate relationships are protected by the Fourteenth Amendment. Please refer to Lawrence, 539 U.S. at 578 and supra, at 23. Later, the Court used the same set of precedents to grant same-sex marriage constitutional recognition. Obergefell, 576 U.S. 665, 666; supra, at 23. In conclusion, decades of precedent about the meaning of the Fourteenth Amendment are intricately entwined with Roe and Casey. Voir supra, pp. 21–24. Roe and Casey are the exact opposite of "'obsolete constitutional reasoning,'" notwithstanding what the majority may prefer. Felton, 521 U.S. 203, 236 (1997) Agostini v. (quoting Casey, 505 U. S., at 857).

Furthermore, Roe and Casey haven't been called into question by further factual developments. Unexpected pregnancy outcomes and unplanned pregnancies continue to affect women. Pregnancy still has significant physical, social, and financial repercussions. Even a simple pregnancy puts a lot of burden on the body since it always involves major physiological change and agonizing pain. Pregnancy and delivery may result in severe physical conditions that may have a fatal outcome for some women. As was already said, nowadays, the dangers of having an abortion pale in comparison to those of bringing a pregnancy to term. Voir supra, p. 22. According to experts, a restriction on abortion raises maternal mortality by 21%, with white women's death increasing by 13% and black women's mortality increasing by 33%. Large-scale financial expenditures are sometimes associated with pregnancy and delivery. The majority briefly discusses the reasons in favor of changing the legislation in regards to family leave, pregnancy discrimination, and healthcare coverage. ante, pp. 33–34.

However, many pregnant women still lack access to proper healthcare coverage, and even when it is offered, access to healthcare facilities may be limited. In addition, prejudice against pregnant women still exists, which hinders their ability to find work. Many people who need paid family leave the most still cannot receive it. Only 20% of employees in the private sector, including only 8% of those in the poorest quartile of wage earners, have access to paid family leave.

The majority briefly mentions the rising desire for adoption and the frequency of safe haven legislation (see ante, at 34, and nn. 45–46), but to the extent that these developments even exist, they are also unimportant. Neither lessens the financial or physical risks associated with pregnancy and delivery.

Furthermore, choosing not to bring a pregnancy to term is quite different from choosing to renounce parental rights after giving birth. Few women who are refused abortions really seek adoption. Like in Roe and Casey's time, the great majority will still be responsible for paying for child care. They will suffer the severe loss of autonomy and dignity that forced pregnancy and delivery always inflict, whether or not they want to become parents.

Despite the majority's claimed "contemporary changes," Mississippi's own history shows how little the reality has changed since Roe and Casey. At 33, ante. Mississippi does not require insurance to cover contraceptives and forbids educators from showing safe contraceptive usage, despite the fact that sixty-two percent of births there are unplanned.

The State does not prohibit pregnancy discrimination or mandate paid parental leave. Brief for National Women's Law Center et al. as Amici Curiae 32; Brief for Yale Law School Information Society Project as Amicus Curiae 13 (Brief for Yale Law School).

It has stringent Medicaid and nutrition assistance qualifying standards, leaving many women and families without access to basic medical care or sufficient food. 547 Deans, Chairs, Scholars, Public Health Professionals, and others, Brief for Amici Curiae 32–34 (Brief for 547 Deans). Despite the fact that postpartum problems account for 86 percent of pregnancy-related fatalities in the state, Mississippi turned down federal financing for a program that would have given new mothers a year of Medicaid coverage. See Yale Law School Brief 12–13. Perhaps not unexpectedly, both women's and children's health results in Mississippi are atrocious.

Mississippi has among of the highest rates of preterm delivery, low birthweight, cesarean section, and maternal death in the nation as well as the highest infant mortality rate. In the State, carrying a pregnancy to term is almost 75 times riskier for a woman than having an abortion. See Brief for Deans 9–10 at 547. We do not claim that every State provides the same level of assistance for women and children as Mississippi, but we are certain that some have improved since Roe and Casey. However, a state-by-state review by public health experts reveals that the States with the strictest abortion laws also continue to make the smallest investments in the health of women and children. See Brief for Deans 23–34 in 547.

The only significant shift since Roe and Casey is that American abortion legislation is more in line with that of other countries, rather than cutting against precedent. The majority, along with the Mississippi Legislature, asserts that when it comes to abortion legislation, the United States is a glaring anomaly. Voir ante, at 6, and n.

But there has been a worldwide trend toward greater accessibility to safe and legal abortion services. Abortions are legal in a few of nations, including New Zealand, the Netherlands, and Iceland, up to a period that is essentially equivalent to the Roe and Casey threshold. See pages 18–22 of the Brief for Scholars of International and Comparative Law as Amici Curiae. Any stage of pregnancy may now be aborted without being punished in Canada. Id., pp. 13–15. The majority of Western European nations prohibit abortion beyond 12 to 14 weeks, although they often provide permissive exceptions, such as when a woman's physical or mental health is at risk. See id., at 24-27; Amici Curiae Brief of European Law Professors, at 16–17; Appendix.

They often facilitate access to early abortions as well, for instance, by contributing to the expense. Perhaps most notably, access to abortion has increased in more than 50 nations worldwide in the last 25 years, including those in Asia, Latin America, Africa, and Europe. See pages 28–29 of the Brief for Scholars of International and Comparative Law as Amici Curiae. The American States will now be considered international outliers due to the global relaxation of abortion legislation.

In conclusion, the majority's judgment cannot be justified by either factual or legal advances. Nothing that has occurred recently in this nation or throughout the globe disproves Roe and Casey's central thesis. It is nevertheless true that, within the parameters of those choices made, a woman should decide whether she will shoulder the responsibilities of pregnancy, delivery, and parenting—not the government.

2

The majority cites two landmark decisions that overturned earlier constitutional precedents, West Coast Hotel Co. v. Parrish and Brown v. Board of Education, in support of its conclusion, see ante, at 40. But unlike today's judgments, previous ones were made in response to altered laws, as well as altered realities and social mores. As Casey acknowledged, the two instances are only pertinent to demonstrate, in striking contrast, how irrational it is to eliminate the freedom to choose. Refer to 505 U.S. at 861–864.

Adkins v. Children's Hospital of D.C., 261 U.S. 525 (1923), and a string of decisions dating back to Lochner v. New York, 198 U. S. 45, were both overturned by West Coast Hotel (1905). A state minimum wage statute had been declared unconstitutional by Adkins because, in the Court's opinion, it interfered with the ability to contract. 261 U.

S., at 554-555. Then, however, came the Great Depression, which brought with it a level of financial misery unlike any other. The event cast doubt on Adkins' belief that a completely unrestrained market could satisfy fundamental human needs—indeed, it contradicted that belief.

The earlier era of laissez-faire was acknowledged to be dead everywhere outside the Court, as Justice Jackson (then a candidate for the position of Justice) wrote of that period. The Fight for Supreme Judicial Power 85 (1941). In West Coast Hotel, the Court caught up, seeing the shortcomings of preexisting legal theory through the prism of experience. also see ante, at 11 (ROBERTS, C. J., concurring in judgment). The Court said that it was "general knowledge across the length and breadth of the nation" how badly the Depression had affected average Americans. 300 U. S., at 399. "The exploitation of employees at salaries so low as to be inadequate to pay the basic cost of life" had resulted from the laissez-faire philosophy. Ibid. Additionally, the law has evolved since the Adkins ruling.

The Court had begun to acknowledge in a number of rulings that States had the authority to enact economic measures that would improve the financial security of their inhabitants. See, for instance, O'Gorman & Young, Inc. v. Hartford Fire Ins. Co., 282 U. S. 251 and Nebbia v. New York, 291 U. S. 502 (1934). (1931). West Coast Hotel said that it was "difficult to reconcile" the comments in those rulings with Adkins. 300 U. S., at 398. Adkins had to go, and there was no getting around it.

Brown v. Board of Education invalidated the "separate but equal" tenet of Plessy v. Ferguson, 163 U. S. 537 (1896). By 1954, years of Jim Crow had made it evident what Plessy's choice of words—"inherent[]

[in]equal[ity]"—really meant. 347 U.S. at 495; Brown.

Segregation is incompatible with the Reconstruction Amendments, which were passed to provide freed slaves full citizenship. The Brown Court said that regardless of what may have been believed during Plessy's time, experience and "contemporary authority" demonstrated the "detrimental effect[s]" of state-sanctioned segregation: It "affected [children's] hearts and minds in a manner unlikely ever to be undone." 347 U. S., at 494.

By then, the legislation had also started to reflect this thinking. The Court has ruled in a number of instances that the barring of black students from public graduate institutions was unconstitutional. See, for instance, Missouri ex rel. Gaines v. Canada, 305 U. S. 337; Sipuel v. Board of Regents of University of Oklahoma, 332 U. S. 631 (1948) (per curiam); Sweatt v. Painter, 339

U. S. 629 (1950); (1938). According to Brown, the reasoning behind such decisions "applied with increased force to youngsters in elementary and high schools." 347 U. S., at 494. Plessy had to terminate because of revised facts and revised legislation.

According to the majority, by acknowledging such developments, we are essentially endorsing the 50-year period between Plessy and Brown. Ante is at 70. This is untrue. First off, whether it was five, fifty, or five hundred years later, the Brown Court may never have reversed Plessy if it had used the majority's theory of constitutional interpretation.

Brown believed that it was "[at] best... inconclusive" whether or not the desegregation-supporting history of the ratification period. 347 U. S., at 489. Even yet, we are not suggesting that a judgment cannot ever be overturned if it is demonstrably incorrect. For example, the majority also cites West Virginia Bd. of Ed. v. Barnette, 319 U. S. 624. Voir ante, p. 40–41, p. 70. Three years after the first judgment, and before any major reliance interests had emerged, that overturning occurred.

Additionally, it occurred because some Justices had a change of heart rather than because a new majority sought to overturn earlier rulings. Additionally, Barnette and Brown have one additional thing in common that sets them distinct from the Court's decision today.

They did not, as the majority does here, take away a right that people have held and depended on for 50 years. Instead, they preserved individual rights with a solid foundation in the Constitution's most basic provisions.

To take such move based on the determination of a fresh and thin majority that two Courts gravely miscalculated the outcome? And to use Barnette as evidence to support that action? Or to Brown, a case where the Chief Justice also penned an opinion (11 pages long) that allowed the Court as a whole to speak with one voice? These queries are self-explanatory.

Casey ruled that neither West Coast Hotel nor Brown agreed with Roe's finding when it addressed both of them. The "facts of economic life" at the West Coast Hotel, according to Casey, had turned out to be "different from those previously assumed." 505 U. S., at 862. Even if "Plessy was erroneous the day it was determined," time has only served to make it more obvious to the public: "Society's knowledge of the facts" in 1954 was "fundamentally different" than it was in 1896. Id., at 863.

The Court had to change its course as a result. As in other areas of life, changing circumstances may impose new duties in constitutional adjudication. Id., at 864. And since there had been such a significant shift, the general people could comprehend why the Court was acting. The Nation "may embrace each ruling" as "the Court's constitutional obligation," according to the statement. Ibid. However, a Roe reversal would not be accurate since "[n]either the factual basis for Roe's basic finding nor our perception of it has altered." 505 U. S., at 864.

That still holds true now since Roe and Casey continue to reflect broad trends in American culture rather than deviate from them. Of course, many Americans, including many women, disagreed with those rulings when they were made and still do now. However, it cannot be denied that Roe and Casey were the result of a significant and continuous shift in women's responsibilities in the later half of the 20th century.

Twelve years before to Roe, the Court said that women were "the center of home and family life," with "unique obligations" that prevented them from having full constitutional protections. Florida v. Hoyt, 368 U.S. 57, 62 (1961). When the Court determined Roe in 1973, substantial societal change affecting the status of women had already started, and the law had started to catch up. 404 U.S. 71, 76 (1971); Reed v. Reed (recognizing that the Equal Protection Clause prohibits sex-based discrimination).

The conventional conception of a woman's duty as merely a wife and mother was "no longer compatible with our understanding of the family, the person, or the Constitution" by 1992, when the Court decided Casey. See supra, at 15, 23 and 24, and 505 U.S., at 897.

Casey was aware that women were required to assume their rightful citizenship status under that charter. Women must have discretion over their reproductive choices in order for it to happen. Nothing has weakened that commitment since Casey—not a changing law, nor a changed truth.

C

The overwhelmingly reliant interests those rulings have generated strengthen the arguments for keeping Roe and Casey. In addition to institutional considerations, the Court follows precedent because it understands that consistency in the law is "an crucial thread in the mantle of protection that the law gives the person." Florida Nursing Home Assn. v. Florida Dept. of Health and Rehabilitative Servs., 450 U. S. 147, 154 (1981) (Stevens, J., concurring).

Therefore, stare decisis has "additional force" because deviating from previous decisions "would unsettle [individuals'] entrenched rights and expectations." South Carolina Public Railways Commission v. Hilton, 502 U. S. 197, 202 (1991). Casey was aware that to "refuse to recognize the fact[s]" was to reject people's dependence on Roe. 505 U. S., at 856.

The bulk of people nowadays reject reality. The lack of any meaningful consideration of how the [majority's] decision would impact women is "the most remarkable element of the [majority]". At 37, ante. It demonstrates how little it understands or cares about the misery its choice would create by referring to Casey's reliance arguments as "generalized generalizations about the national psychology," ante, at 64.

In Casey, the Court noted that people "had arranged personal relationships and made" key life decisions for the last 20 years "in reliance on the availability of abortion in the event that contraceptive should fail." 505 U.

S., at 856. Over the course of another 30 years, that dependency has grown.

According to Casey, "[w]omen's capacity to participate equally in the economic and social life of the Nation has been assisted by their ability to govern their reproductive lives for half a century now." See ante, at 23–24; ibid. In fact, all women who are at reproductive age grew up expecting to be able to take use of Roe's and Casey's safeguards.

Therefore, reversing Roe and Casey will have a significant impact. The medical technique of having an abortion is widespread, and it is a frequent experience for women. A quarter of American women will have an abortion before the age of 45, and around 18% of pregnancies in this nation end in abortions.

Those figures illustrate the expected and profound repercussions of pregnancy, childbirth, and parenthood. As Casey realized, individuals now depend on their capacity to schedule and regulate pregnancies when choosing where and how to live, whether and how to invest in school or employment, how to utilize their financial resources, and how to approach personal and familial relationships. When contraception fails, women may rely on access to abortion.

When contraception is not an option, like as after being raped, they may rely on access to abortion. If anything unexpected happens during a pregnancy, such as a change in family or financial circumstances, unforeseen medical issues, or sad fetal diagnosis, they may turn to abortion as a backup plan. All those personal goals and dreams are destroyed when the majority today takes away the right to an abortion. By doing this, it reduces women's possibilities to take full and equal part in the political, social, and economic life of the country. The availability of abortion "has enormous consequences on women's education, labor force participation, vocations, and wages," as shown in Brief for Economists as Amici Curiae 13

The attitude of the majority to these evident issues is far different from the reality that American women really experience. "Reproductive planning might practically take immediate account of any abrupt reinstatement of governmental power to outlaw abortions," the majority declares. At 64, ante (quoting Casey, 505 U. S., at 856). According to statistics, 45 percent of pregnancies in the US are unintended. Regarding 547 Deans, see the brief. Even the most successful methods of birth control are ineffective, and they are not widely available. Not all sexual relations are voluntary, and not all contraception decisions are made by the partner who runs the risk of becoming pregnant.

Legal Voice et al briefs as amici curiae are included on pages 18–19. For instance, the relevant Mississippi legislation does not include any exceptions for rape or incest, not even for young girls. Last but not least, the majority disregards the fact that some women choose to have an abortion because their circumstances change throughout a pregnancy, as was previously stated. see above, p. 49.

Hopes and plans don't matter much to human bodies. Events that might dramatically affect what it means to carry a pregnancy to term can happen after conception, including unanticipated medical concerns and changes in family circumstances. Women have anticipated in each of these scenarios that they would have the freedom to decide whether to carry a pregnancy to term, maybe with the advice of their relatives or physicians but without government involvement. The loss of Roe and Casey might have terrible consequences for individuals who will now have to experience that pregnancy.

This is particularly true for poor women. It is easy to see where the biggest burden will fall when we "calculate[] the cost of [Roe's] repudiation" on women who previously depended on that ruling. Casey, 505 U. S. 855 Women with money will still be able to go to places that forbid abortion in order to get the treatment they need. The most affected group will be women who cannot afford to do so.

These are the women who are most likely to first seek out abortion services. Nearly half of women who seek abortion care reside in homes that are below the federal poverty line, and unplanned pregnancy rates are five times greater for women in lower income groups than for women in higher income groups. See the briefs for 547 Deans (7), Abortion Funds as Amici Curiae (8), and

Practical Support Organizations (9). (Brief for Abortion Funds).

These women confront significant challenges in gathering the money required to get early-pregnancy abortion treatment, even with Roe's protection. After today, individuals will no longer be able to get safe, legal abortion treatment in States where they are not permitted. They won't have enough money to take the vacation, pay for daycare during that time, or take time off from work. Many people will go through pregnancy and give birth despite not wanting to. Others may resort to risky and illegal abortions out of desperation. They can lose their lives as well as their freedom.

Finally, many women's identities and positions in the society depend on their ability to exercise reproductive control. Casey, 505 U.S. at 856, is cited. This expectation contributes to the definition of a woman as a "equal citizen[]," along with the rights, benefits, and responsibilities such position involves. See supra, at 23–24; Gonzales, 550 U.S. at 172 (Ginsburg, J., dissenting).

It shows that she is a self-sufficient individual who is respected by both society and the law. The freedom to make her own decisions places a woman in relation to other people and the government, as do many other fundamental rights.

It contributes to the definition of a space of freedom where an individual may make decisions without interference from the government. The appropriate "order[s]" Casey's "thinking" and "life," as she realized. 505 U. S., at 856. Her whole existence shows the power and authority that the right confers, regardless of whatever personal decisions she may have made about her place of residence, education, or employment.

Removing a woman's ability to decide whether or not to carry her pregnancy does not imply that no decision is being made. It implies that the States have now been granted this option after being deprived of it by the majority of the current Court.

Allowing a State to have influence over one of a woman's "most private and personal decisions" won't only have a significant impact on how her life turns out. Id., at 851. It is intended to change how she "sees [herself]" and how she perceives her "position in society" as someone with the acknowledged dignity and power to make these decisions. Id., at 856. For 50 years, women have depended on Roe and Casey in this manner. Many people have only ever known one thing. The loss of authority, command, and respect that will occur when Roe and Casey go will be significant.

The Court's limited understanding of reliance may be seen in its inability to recognize the full range of expectations Roe and Casey generated. A reliance interest, in the opinion of the majority, must be "extremely tangible," such as those involving "property" or "contract."

At 64, ante. Casey, 505 U.S. at 855, states that while many of this Court's opinions addressing reliance have been in the "commercial setting," none argues that interests must be comparable to those of businesses in order to qualify for stare decisis protection. This bold claim to authority lies at the core of this extraordinary declaration. The Court grants itself the power to overturn established legal principles by denying the need to take into account the interests of large groups of people. This is done without even acknowledging the costs of the Court's decisions for those who must abide by the law, which this Court's stare decisis doctrine instructs us to give priority when determining whether to change course.

The Court should not take into account the reliance interests that women have in Roe and Casey, according to the majority, even if it were inclined to do so, because they are too "intangible." At 65, ante. This is ignoring what we know about men and women as judges. Women are drawn to Roe and Casey for precisely real, visceral reasons.

Numerous women will now choose differently than they would have when Roe served as a backstop regarding their professions, education, relationships, and whether or not to attempt for a baby. When they might have previously opted to have an abortion, some women will carry their pregnancies to term, with all the expense and risk of injury it entails. Roe and Casey have been essential in granting autonomy over their bodies and lives to millions of women. The misery that today's choice will cause won't go away if we close our eyes to it. By bringing up the "conflicting arguments" of "contending factions," the majority cannot get out of its duty to "consider the cost[s]" of its choice. Casey, 505 U.S. at 855, and ante at 65 According to the principle of stare decisis, those who have depended on a decision should bear the expenses of its repudiation, not those who have disavowed it. Check out Casey, 505 U.S. at 855.

In general, our country's notion of constitutional rights cannot be reconciled with the majority's perspective on dependence. A finding of reliance on a broad range of rulings establishing constitutional rights, such as the freedom to express beliefs, select whom to marry, or pick how to educate children, would be impossible given the majority's emphasis on a "concrete," economic demonstration. According to the rationale of the majority, the Court might transfer such decisions to the State without taking into account a person's established belief that the law makes them hers. It must be incorrect. All of those freedoms, including the right to an abortion, have a significant impact on and even serve as an anchor on people's life. Recognizing that individuals have depended on these rights does not involve engaging in abstract thought; rather, it acknowledges some of the most "real" and well-known facets of freedom and human existence. At 64, ante.

Because of the part that constitutional freedoms play in our system of governance, all of those rights, including this one, also have a social component. See, for instance, Dickerson, 530 U.S. at 443 (refusing to overturn Miranda v. Arizona, 384 U.S. 436 (1966) although acknowledging that Miranda "warnings have become part of our national culture)). All those who have depended on our constitutional form of governance and its framework of individual rights safeguarded from state monitoring are impacted by the Court's historic decision today to completely revoke an individual right and grant it to the State. Of course, Roe and Casey have sparked debate and dissent. However, the rights those rulings granted and upheld are part of how society understands constitutional law and how the Supreme Court has characterized the freedom and equality that women have a right to demand.

Young women will soon reach adulthood with less rights than their moms and grandparents had after today. Most people achieve that outcome without even thinking about how much women have depended on their freedom to choose or what it takes to exercise that choice immediately. A startling indictment of the majority's choice is the fact that it refused to even examine the potentially life-altering effects of overturning Roe and Casey.

D

One last argument works against the majority's decision: the debate surrounding

Roe and Casey itself. In an attempt to prevent "national divisiveness," the majority accuses Casey of forcing an immoral "settlement" of the abortion debate by acting beyond the confines of the law. At 67, Ante.

But Casey didn't act in that way. As was seen above, Casey upheld Roe by using the conventional stare decisis standards that the majority of courts presently disregard. Casey thoroughly evaluated the reliance interests and shifting circumstances (none) (profound). It took into account every facet of Roe's framework's functionality. It conducted its study in accordance with the law and came to the conclusion that the law demanded. It is true that Casey was aware of the "national turmoil" surrounding abortion; the court was aware of this in 1973 as well as 1992. Roe, 410 U.S. at 116; Casey, 505 U.S. at 867-868 Contrary to what the majority implies, Casey's justification for admitting public disagreement was quite different. Casey brought up the national debate to underline how crucial it was for the Court to uphold the law in that case above all others. Wish the majority of today had followed their example.

Think about how the majority describes this facet of Casey:

The American people's faith in the rule of law would be undermined if they ceased to see this Court as a body that renders significant decisions in accordance with principles, not'social and political influences.' When the Court overturns a contentious "watershed" decision like Roe, there is a particular risk that the public may believe the decision was done for unethical motives. It would be seen as a "surrender to political pressure" and "under fire" if a decision was taken to overturn Roe. At 66-67, the ante (citations omitted).

That seems like a decent description to us. And it makes sense to us. The majority replies, "Well, certainly, but we have to apply the law," assuming we interpret them right. Look at ante, at 67. Casey would have responded by saying: "That is precisely the idea."

The Court must apply the law—particularly the rule of stare decisis—here more than anyplace else. Because "men and women of decent conscience" strongly differ over abortion, we may be sure that people will continue to challenge the Court's ruling in this instance. 505 U. S. Casey, at 850. The Court must be firm and hold its position when such contestation occurs but there is no legal justification for changing direction. The rule of law calls for that. And on that, respect for this Court is based.

In such a heated setting, Casey said, "the pledge of constancy, once offered, binds its creator for so long as the knowledge of the subject has not altered so profoundly as to render the commitment outdated." Id., at 868. It is "nothing less than a breach of trust" to break that pledge. Ibid.

"[A]nd No Court could reasonably demand credit for principle if it betrayed its trust with the people." Ibid. No Court would be commended for upholding the law by betraying its trust in such a manner.

In another instance, one of Casey's writers said that in "sensitive political circumstances" where "partisan disagreement abounds," "Our legitimacy demands, above all, that we adhere to stare decisis." 517 U.S. 952, 985 (1996) (O'Connor, J. opinion in Bush v. Vera).

Justice Jackson once referred to a judgment on which he had differed as a "loaded weapon" that may be used improperly. United States v. Korematsu, 323 U. S. 214, 246 (1944). We worry that today's decision, which deviates from stare decisis without good cause, is a self-fulfilling prophecy. Beyond any one ruling, a weakened stare decisis threated to overturn fundamental legal principles. Significant legal instability results from weakening stare decisis.

Furthermore, as Casey noted, undermining stare decisis in a contentious case like this one raises concerns about the Court's adherence to legal principles. It gives the Court the appearance of being unrestrained yet forceful, unassuming but clingy. We worry that today's ruling undermines the rule of law in all those ways.

The new currency of this Court's decision-making is power, not reason. 844 in Payne, 501 U.S. (Marshall, J., dissenting). Roe has been standing for 50 years. Casey, a precedent that expressly confirms Roe has been upheld for thirty years. And the stare decisis theory, which is a foundational principle of the rule of law, firmly supports their continuous existence. The right those rulings created and upheld is ingrained in our constitution's legislation, emerging from and paving the way for other rights safeguarding one's physical integrity, individual freedom, and familial ties.

The right to an abortion is also deeply ingrained in the lives of women, impacting their expectations, dating and career decisions, and promoting (as do other reproductive rights) their social and economic equality. Nothing has changed since the right was acknowledged (and affirmed) in order to continue supporting what the majority does now. Law, facts, and attitudes have not offered any additional justifications for arriving at a different conclusion than Roe and Casey did. Only this Court has undergone any alteration.

Mississippi—as well as other States—knew precisely what they were doing when they sparked fresh legal disputes against Roe and

Casey. The 15-week restriction in question was passed into law in 2018. Other nations soon followed: Eight States outlawed abortion treatments beyond six to eight weeks of pregnancy between 2019 and 2021, while three States passed outright bans.

Mississippi determined that it had not gone far enough in 2019: The State enacted a 6-week limitation a year after the statute under review was approved. The supporter of both Mississippi bills, a state senator, said the obvious aloud. Many individuals, he said, "felt that now that we had" a conservative Court, it would be a good idea to start challenging Roe's boundaries. The State had shown a little caution in its petition for certiorari. It clearly assured the Court that "the concerns posed in this petition do not compel the Court to reject" those decisions when it requested the Court to simply reverse Roe and Casey. Petition for Cert. No. 5; ante, at 5–6 (ROBERTS, C. J., concurring in judgment). But Mississippi decided to go all in as it became more and more optimistic about its possibilities. It requested that the Court reject Roe and Casey. The only thing that would suffice is everything.

This Court gave a hint earlier in the term that Mississippi's plan might work. A small number of States, including Texas, recently outlawed abortions after six weeks of pregnancy. It added an extraordinary plan to "evade judicial scrutiny" to that limitation that was "clearly unlawful." Jackson, 594 U. S., 2021 (SOTOMAYOR, J., dissenting) Whole Woman's Health (slip op., at 1). And five Justices agreed to such shady ploy. They allowed Texas to disregard the constitutional judgments of this Court, thus overturning Roe and Casey earlier than expected in the nation's second-largest State.

And thanks to that same five-person majority, the second shoe has now dropped.

(We think THE CHIEF JUSTICE's judgment is incorrect as well, but no one should assume that there is not a significant difference between enabling States to outlaw abortion beginning at conception and maintaining a 15-week ban on the grounds he does.) Now, a new and slim majority of this Court overrules Roe and Casey, moving virtually as soon as it can.

It transforms a number of dissident views opposing Roe and Casey into a ruling supporting even outright abortion prohibitions. 57, 59, 63, and nn in ante, pages 61–64 (relying on former dissents). It repeals a 50-year-old constitutional provision that protects women's equality and freedom. It violates a fundamental rule-of-law concept intended to support legal consistency. All of that compromises other rights, including those to marriage, same-sex intimacy, and contraception. Finally, it jeopardizes the credibility of the Court.

Even if part in its majority may not have first agreed with Roe, Casey itself provided the final argument for why it would not overturn Roe. Casey outlined the significance of stare decisis, the inappropriateness of West Coast Hotel and Brown, and the lack of any "new circumstances" (or other cause) that would have justified the overturning of precedent, exactly as we did here. ; see ante, at 30-33, 37-47; 505 U.S., at 864.

The Supreme Court "could not pretend," according to Casey, that overturning Roe had any "justification beyond a contemporary doctrinal propensity to come out differently from the Court of 1973." 505 U. S., at 864. And to override because of that? Casey quoted Justice Stewart in saying that doing so would lead people to believe that "this institution is little different from the two political branches of the Government" and that precedent should not be overturned "on a ground no firmer than a change in [the Court's] membership." Ibid. No viewpoint, in Casey's opinion, could "more permanently harm this Court and the legal system that it is our abiding mission to serve." Ibid. Casey concluded that the Court would pay a "terrible price" for overturning Roe. 505 U. S., at 864.

Justices O'Connor, Kennedy, and Souter were wise justices when they penned those lines. The kind of ideological purity that some court observers expect Justices to exhibit, however, would have eliminated them from any competition. If there were prizes for Justices who left this Court in better shape than when they arrived, though? And who, as a result, left our nation in a better position? And is the rule of law more solid? Register those Justices.

They were aware that "the Court's legitimacy [is] acquired through time." Id., at 868. They would also have understood how much more rapidly it may be destroyed. To prevent such a result in Casey, they put up a lot of effort. They believed that the American people should never believe that their constitutional rights were in jeopardy and that a new majority, subscribing to a new "doctrinal school," could "by force of numbers" alone revoke them. Id., at 864. It is challenging—no, it is impossible—to draw any other conclusions from this situation. "[I]t is not often in the law that so few have so swiftly altered so much," one of us once stated.

Breaking the Promise of Brown: The Resegregation of American Schools by S. Breyer (2022). That has never been more true for all of us in our tenure on this Court than it is right now.

We dissented out of sadness, not only for this Court but also for the countless millions of American women who have now lost a crucial constitutional safeguard.

SUMMARY

As of today, 25th August 2022, many states have given their ruling on whether or not abortion should be legalised. Many disagreed and few have agreed to legalizing abortion with it's reason being the right and choice of a woman. Personally from my own standing, I believe abortion shouldn't be legalized. Taking the life of a child who cannot speak for itself is nothing short of heartless. You do not want children? Use contraceptives or abstain from intercourse. But in a situation where one conceives mistakenly, I'd advice that the child is welcomed with utmost loved and taken care of with 💯 care and responsibility.

While many may disagree, this is my own standing. It is Biblically wrong to kill a child.